AWAKENING TO ONE LOVE

Praise for *Awakening to One Love*

In *Awakening to One Love*, Beth Geer has given us a profound treasure... the invitation and opportunity to awaken from the suffering of ego identification to the highest, truest aspect of our being... Oneness. Beth translates the wisdom from *"A Course In Miracles"* into everyday language. This book is an insightful, mind-expanding guide from fears and limiting beliefs, to the Truth that eternal peace, love and joy is merely a perception shift away. Reading this book mindfully is an effective and efficient way to re-focus your awareness word by word until you are anchored in the highest Truth and magnificence of who and what you really are. *Awakening to One Love* will no doubt raise your consciousness and vibration. Give yourself this gift and experience the freedom and expansion that comes from growing and evolving as a body, mind and soul.

Eric J. Christopher, MSMFT, CHT
Marriage & Family Therapist; Certified Hypnotherapist
www.ericjchristopher.com

There are no coincidences; you are in the right place. If you're attracted to this book then buy it! What I love most about this book is that you can benefit in at least three different ways. Beth gives you a blueprint of how you can directly connect to Source... simply do what she did. Get ALL the powerful wisdom lessons from *A Course in Miracles* right here. Use this book as a companion guide, to dive deep into *A Course in Miracles*.
I not only love the content of this book, but how it was birthed!

Daniel D'Neuville
Founder and Principal, D'Neuville Training Group
Area Coordinator, DFW Chapter of the Institute of Noetic Sciences
daniel@dfwions.org

Communicating with Spirit from within. I've done it for miles on Colorado's High Country hiking trails. Beth connected through her study of *The Course of Miracles*. Beth captured her conversations. I didn't! This is a beautiful, insightful and inspirational conversation with Source. Invaluable for anyone on a spiritual journey, regardless of where you are on yours. Highly recommend!

Thomas Miller, Author
Audiobook Narrator & Host "Subconscious Mind Mastery" Podcast

AWAKENING TO ONE LOVE

Uncover the inner peace and joy hidden within you

BETH GEER

COGENT
PUBLISHING NY
IMPRINT OF
THE WHITSON GROUP, INC.

Published by Cogent Publishing NY
Imprint of The Whitson Group, Inc.
3 Miller Road, Putnam Valley, NY 10579
(845) 528-7617 • www.cogentpub.com
cogentpub@aol.com

Art on front cover by Kenneth Laugen, Trondheim, Norway

ISBN: 978-0-925776-48-8
1 2 3 4 5—21 20 19 18

This book is dedicated to the Holy Spirit within each of us.
Thank You for being Our Answer from God.

*"An unheard message will not save the world, however mighty
be the Voice that speaks, however loving the message be."*
A COURSE IN MIRACLES: LESSON 123:5-6

Acknowledgements

I would like to thank every single soul in existence—you who are the Extensions of my One Self, forever held with me in the eternal moment of now, in Total Love and Peace. Together we are One Love, strong in our Perfect Unity with our Creator; and I am absolutely grateful that this, and nothing else, is true. I extend my deepest gratitude to each and every one of you, for being exactly Who You Are.

More specifically I would like to thank my husband Paul, for your unwavering support, loving patience, and endless technical help. You denied me nothing throughout this entire process. Without you, this book would not exist, and I am eternally grateful.

I would also like to thank my dear editors Michael Fragnito and Ronnie Whitson, and my agent Ivor Whitson. From the very beginning, the Holy Spirit promised to send me only the best help, and He delivered on that promise. Together, you brought this book to fruition.

And last but far from least, I would like to thank my artist and dear friend Kenneth Laugen whose world-renowned work graces the cover of my book. Somehow the Holy Spirit brought us together, even though you live halfway around the world in Norway. The story of how our friendship came to be is something of a miracle, arranged by the Holy Spirit no doubt. Kenneth, I am so deeply honored to have your award winning, highly acclaimed artwork shine on the cover of my book.

And I thank you Holy Spirit, for all whom you sent me. I know I have been sent nothing but angels.

Do not miss this message.
Be willing to open your eyes to see, and your ears to hear.

Never forget to forgive.
If you do forget,
Then it is never too late to forgive.
Above all else,
Forgive.

(First advice given to me by the Holy Spirit within.)

AWAKENING TO ONE LOVE

Table of Contents

Preface

Each of us contains an Inner Voice, a Guide, a Helper Who speaks to us from a sacred space within. For most of us, this Voice lies deep within the recesses of our mind, unnoticed, unheard, denied, and buried. This Inner Voice has gone by many names, and some who have managed to hear It have written about the wisdom they've received. In the pages that follow, I hope to share conversations with you from my own inner journey with this Voice, and the profound messages I received. These conversations center around the Workbook lessons from a book called *A Course in Miracles*. They deal with our everyday individual problems, and the world at large.

I was drawn to meditation and communion with "the power beyond me" at an early age. I've always prayed, but by the time I was a teenager, I began actively seeking two-way communication with God, or Whomever must have created me. I knew I did not make myself, and I had questions about that. Where did I really come from? Why am I here? What does God want from me anyway?

It was through seeking answers to these questions that I was drawn to *A Course in Miracles* sometime in 2004. The book is divided into three parts. The first part is a 669-page section referred to as the TEXT. It took me almost nine years to get through this part, largely due to the fact that I would set the book aside for days, weeks, and sometimes even months at a time. I did this because I had almost no comprehension of what I read within its pages, and found I couldn't read it at a faster pace. But stubbornly, I kept at it; hoping I'd understand it in time. I at least recognized the divine importance of the words, though I had little idea as to their meaning.

Fast forward nine years to 2013 when I began reading the second section called the WORKBOOK FOR STUDENTS. This section is comprised of 365 daily lessons based on the material from the TEXT. The reader is instructed to do no more than one lesson per day, but more than one day may be spent per lesson. The lessons themselves are comprised of spiritual teachings on peace, love and forgiveness, which the reader is to learn to incorporate into their daily lives. I finished it in exactly one year, not missing a single day, then moved on to part three: the MANUAL FOR TEACHERS. This section is comprised of material intended to help answer questions and clarify terms from the Course teachings. I finished its 72 pages in just a few months.

I felt my understanding of this enigmatic work had only inched forward after reading every single word within its pages. By this time it was now 2015, and I decided to try the 365 daily Workbook lessons for the second time around. It was at the beginning of my second attempt at these lessons that my inner ears opened wide to the Voice within me.

This Voice is never judgmental, cruel, or deprecating. He is never negative. He has always, and will forever be, wholly loving, forgiving, and kind. I believe this Voice is none other than the Holy Spirit Himself, Who dwells within every single one of us.

I've been asked: "How do you know this Voice isn't just a fabrication of your own imagination? How do you know you're not just crazy?"

The answer is: I don't know. Is this Inner Voice only me, or truly the Holy Spirit? Is it both of us, or neither? I have no way of proving anything to myself, much less to anyone else. All I can ask myself is this: Has the Voice been loving, helpful and kind to me? Yes, of that much I am certain. And that much I can share with you in order that you, dear reader, may decide for yourself. I can also say that I am frequently surprised by His answers; feeling as though I couldn't have come up with them on my own, and many of His ideas are entirely new to me. The rest I must take on faith alone.

That being said, I want to emphasize the fact that I am in no way more special than anyone else for hearing Him. He speaks to all of us, but few choose to listen. The lessons in this book are aimed at teaching you how to listen, in order that you too, may hear Him and consciously benefit from His loving Guidance. We all carry His Voice within us, and we can all learn to hear Him once again. We have simply chosen to block our inner ears to His Voice. The good news is, this choice can be unmade.

This whole experience came about as I sat down in 2015 to attempt the Workbook lessons for the second time, feeling deeply frustrated. I read the first lesson and thought, "I still don't know what this means, and I've read this book cover to cover now. I must be the worst student ever. I'm failing this course."

To my surprise, the Voice of the Holy Spirit clearly answered me. *"You are not the worst student ever,"* He replied. *"No one understands My lessons right away. And no one can fail My Course."*

At first, I couldn't believe that me of all people, would be lucky enough to be in contact with the Holy Spirit. In fact, I didn't truly believe it for a long time. I felt as though I was just "playing along," being a good sport, listening, and taking down notes on what He said about each lesson. But after some time, I realized there was no way these answers were coming from my own imagination. They were coming from somewhere Divine, beyond my small mind.

At one point I asked, "Why me? Why are You giving me all this extra help? Am I such a remedial student that I need such special assistance?"

His only reply was, *"Because you asked. Then listened for My answer."*

And so, the Holy Spirit and I went through each daily lesson together over the course of a year, as He explained each one to me in the simplest of terms. I felt as though I had my own tutor.

Along the way, I also asked many questions about life, our purpose here, and the world in general. Our discussions were candid, and I held nothing back. I have incorporated these questions into a Q&A format at the end of each section of lessons. The Holy Spirit answered all of my questions within the context of the Course teachings; explaining how this information can be used to heal our individual and global problems.

I have no control over the Voice of the Holy Spirit. I only know that I cannot hear Him if He is not invited by me. Learning how to offer this invitation has taken some practice. Some days, the answers to my questions would come as I read the lesson itself. At other times, the dialogue would happen suddenly while folding laundry, washing the dishes, while driving, or at work. The key element to my hearing Him always seemed to be when I was in a state of inner peace. I didn't have to spend hours meditating in the lotus position, attend any type of class, or go to any special place. Our conversations would happen when I was at peace with what I was doing in the present moment; going about the ordinary daily tasks I always do. The task didn't seem to matter so much as the level of peace my heart slipped into while doing it. And so it was, that at times, the Holy Spirit would speak to me all through the day.

I refer to this Inner Voice as the Holy Spirit and as a male, only because I am most comfortable with this. I believe He presents Himself to us in the form we can most easily accept without fear, and for me that's as a loving father. I don't truly believe God has any gender or form; He is beyond all words or form. I am simply most comfortable speaking about Him using the male pronoun, and referring to Him as the Holy Spirit. Please keep an open mind, and take no offense at this. You may decide you hear God, Jesus or another Divine Voice. Call Him whatever you'd like. It does not matter. Recognition of the Voice within doesn't come from the title you assign Him. Recognition comes from the consistently loving message He delivers to you.

We are all traveling this path together, on the same journey, towards the same happy destination; the remembrance of our Union in God. There are many ways to learn to regain this memory, and hear His Voice once again. I aim to share one of those ways in the pages that follow.

Introduction

So what is *A Course in Miracles?*

The book was scribed by Dr. Helen Schucman, Professor of Medical Psychology, over the course of seven years, beginning sometime in 1965. She claimed the "Voice" she was listening to, was none other than Jesus Christ Himself. The book was first published in June of 1975 by the Foundation for Inner Peace, the organization specifically chosen by Dr. Schucman for this purpose. Since then it has been translated by the Foundation into over twenty-seven languages and is studied by thousands of students worldwide.

Helen Schucman seemed an unlikely candidate for this important job. But such is the way of God, that He at times chooses those of us who appear the least appropriate to carry out His Work. As it turned out, Helen was perfect for the task, despite her personal beliefs.

She was anything but spiritual—a self-described atheist in fact. I believe that this very atheism is what cleared a space within her mind where new beliefs in a kind and loving God might take root. Below, in Helen's own words, is a brief self description of the momentous moments that precipitated the book's scribing:

"Psychologist, educator, conservative in theory and atheistic in belief, I was working in a prestigious and highly academic setting. And something happened that triggered a chain of events I could never have predicted. The head of my department unexpectedly announced that he was tired of the angry and aggressive feelings our attitudes reflected, and concluded that "there must be another way." As if on cue, I agreed to help him find it. Apparently this Course is the other way." (ACIM-Preface)

The "head of her department" (with whom she did not get along at the time), was fellow Professor of Medical Psychology, William Thetford, who eventually would type the words from Helen's notes and help her compile the book. It was their willingness to peaceably join together in a common purpose that triggered Jesus to enter, and a healing between them to begin. Theirs was a common problem we all have; two people who don't see eye to eye, who either need to find another way, (a better, more loving way) or continue to suffer. The choice is always ours.

Soon after this agreement, Helen, for three months began to receive highly symbolic, spiritual dreams. It appeared as though her mind was being prepared, or "healed" enough to become a better "receiver" for what Jesus was about to reveal to her. Although she had grown accustomed to the unexpected by that time, at one point she was very surprised when she one day wrote: "This is a course in miracles." (ACIM-Preface)

That was her introduction to the "Voice" as she initially called it. (It took her a long time before she actually, personally and publicly, came to accept it was Jesus speaking to her). The Voice didn't come to her audibly, but rather, as a rapid "inner dictation," which she wrote down in a notebook. She could pause this Voice anytime, go about her normal daily life, and then pick up her dictation again later without any difficulty.

The names of all the collaborators, including Helen's, are not included on the cover of the Course, as no one felt they could claim to be its author. Helen herself only ever claimed to be its scribe.

The Course itself was not written for, nor intended as, the start of another religion or cult. Its only purpose is to provide a clear way in which *some* people will be best able to find and hear their own Internal Teacher.

In the chapters that follow, I will be taking you on a journey through the 365 daily lessons from the WORKBOOK FOR STUDENTS, combined with associated passages from the TEXT, as they were explained to me by the Holy Spirit. This material can be difficult to understand at first, and many students struggle with it. It is my hope that the clarification I received from the Holy Spirit will help others understand the profound healing message contained within the pages of *A Course in Miracles*.

I have posed the questions of "Why am I writing this book? Why now?" to the Holy Spirit. He replied: *"Many people are in your same predicament; feeling frustrated and confused about My message as presented in the Course. This book will serve as an intermediary step bridging the gap between confusion and total understanding. I will explain the truth to you as even a child can understand, in order that greater learning may be achieved with the Course itself."*

The need for this message of truth to be expressed in a variety of ways through other teachers is clearly stated within the Course itself:

"Are other teachers possible, to lead the way to those who speak in different tongues and appeal to different symbols? Certainly there are. Would God leave anyone without a very present help in time of trouble; a savior who can symbolize Himself? Yet do we need a many-faceted curriculum, not because of content differences, but because symbols must shift and change to suit the need. Jesus has come to answer yours. In him you find God's Answer." (MANUAL-23.7:2-7)

As long as the content of the message remains the same, it does not matter how or from whom it is delivered.

However, I cannot emphasize enough that I feel the Course is already complete unto itself and doesn't need any extra help from me to expand upon its meaning. It is not my intention to re-write or improve upon it in any way. I am only sharing the message of the Course in its simplest possible form as explained to me by the Holy Spirit, so that others may benefit as I have.

For ease in following the dialogue between the Holy Spirit and myself, I will delineate my own words as "ME" and the words I received from the Holy Spirit as "HS."

Referencing *A Course in Miracles*

A Course in Miracles (the Course) is divided into three main parts—TEXT, WORKBOOK FOR STUDENTS, MANUAL FOR TEACHERS and CLARIFICATION OF TERMS. In addition it contains a Preface and two Supplements—PSYCHOTHERAPY: PURPOSE, PROCESS AND PRACTICE, and SONG OF PRAYER.

References to quotes and excerpts from the Course are included throughout this book to facilitate finding where in the book they appear.

Parts of the Course as shown in the references

T- references TEXT
W- references WORKBOOK FOR STUDENTS
M- references MANUAL FOR TEACHERS
P- references PSYCHOTHERAPY
S- references SONG OF PRAYER

For all references the part is designated first, followed by chapter or lesson number, section, then sub-section. These are followed by the paragraph number and sentence number/s within the paragraph. For example, T-5.IV.3;2:5-6 references TEXT-chapter 5.section IV.subsection 3.paragraph 2:sentences 5-6.

You may notice that lesson numbers appear to skip in places. This is because some lessons, not included here, are repeated a second time within Review sections.

All quotes are from *A Course in Miracles* (ACIM), Third Edition, 2007, used with written permission from its original publisher, the Foundation for Inner Peace, which was specifically chosen by Dr. Helen Schucman to publish the Course.

Chapter 1: Lessons 1-5

This Is Not The Real World

Lesson 1. Nothing I see in this room [on this street, from this window, in this place] means anything.

ME: I still don't know what this means, and I've read this book cover to cover now. I'm must be the worst student ever. I'm failing this course.

HS: You are *not* the worst student ever. No one understands My lessons right away. And no one can fail My Course.

ME: Um. Okay. I'll just take Your word for it. So, why does "nothing I see mean anything?" What do You mean by that?

HS: The first lessons make more sense when taken together as a group. Even then, they are initially abstract for your concrete mind. This is why the review of the first fifty lessons are placed together in groups of five. Please take down these first five lessons, and I will show you how they all make sense, once fitted together.

ME: Alright.

1. Nothing I see in this room [on this street, from this window, in this place] means anything.

HS: The world you see with your physical eyes is not the real world. It is an illusion, a place of separation you made in an attempt to escape from God. Everything you see with your physical eyes is susceptible to time and degradation, which means it is not real. If it were real, it could be taken with you into Heaven. Only the eternal is real and only the eternal can pass on into Heaven, and only God can create what is eternal. Therefore, nothing you see in this world is real, and being unreal (lacking eternal qualities) it has no more meaning than a child's make-believe world. And just like a child, you have given everything you see in this world all the meaning that is has for you.

9

2. I have given everything I see in this room
[on this street, from this window, in this place]
all the meaning that it has for me.

HS: God gave you His power to create, when He created you. All you look upon with your bodily eyes is an illusion of fear you've made with His power. Because nothing you see is the real, you do not truly understand what the world looks like in truth; what it looks like when not covered by your illusions.

3. I do not understand anything I see in this room
[on this street, from this window, in this place].

HS: You think you see a real world. You believe wholeheartedly in the illusion you've cast. It fills every sense in your body, and so it fills your mind with only what you think about the illusion you live in. You know nothing about the reality that lies just beyond this one.

4. These thoughts do not mean anything.
They are like the things I see in this room
[on this street, from this window, in this place.]

HS: Your thoughts do not mean anything, because your mind is filled with things that are not real. Your mind is filled with thoughts about a world that does not exist in truth.

5. I am never upset for the reason I think.

HS: You think you are upset about the happenings outside of you in the world you see. Yet, all your fear, pain, anxiety and frustrations arise from an inner guilt; a feeling you don't want to be here. In truth, you're upset because of a choice you made from within; the choice to come here to begin with. You are never upset for the reason you think.

. . .

ME: That's a lot to take in. So if nothing I see outside myself is real, then how am I supposed to react to the illusion all around me? Walk around pretending I don't see the world?

HS: No. You look directly at it, and forgive it.

ME: Forgive it?

HS: Yes. You forgive yourself for seeing all Life as separated. Separate objects, separate bodies, and separate minds. It causes you endless anxiety, fear, anger, and depression to see the world as separated. It is un-natural for Whole eternal beings such as yourselves to exist in a finite world of separation. Forgive yourself for imagining it is so. Forgive yourself the tiny mistake of deciding to see yourself as separate from Me.

ME: That's certainly a different way of looking at the world.

HS: It is. In fact, it is the total opposite of how you've been taught to see the world since birth, and this is why you resist. If you saw all things as One, your memory of Me would be instantly restored. Then the world as you know it would disappear, replaced by the real one God Created. You would immediately see Heaven.

ME: What? That sounds like entering another dimension. That thought is a bit terrifying actually.

HS: You fear Heaven while clinging to the hell you're currently living in. It is the reversal of this very thinking that I aim to help you with.

ME: Thought reversal doesn't sound as terrifying as dimension shifting. And You're right. We're all born with amnesia, aren't we? We can't remember a darn thing from before we were born. Why *did* You take our memories away anyway?

HS: I did not take them away. You gave them up. Voluntarily. Because of this, none of you can remember anything from the time before you were born into this world. You do not remember the state of peace, love, and wholeness of your mind before you seemingly split off from Me to come into this illusion. The memory of your Perfect Union is what these lessons aim to restore to your split minds. The goal of this Course, is to heal all your pain and suffering completely.

ME: Why would we ever do that? Why would we voluntarily give up our memory of You in an attempt to separate?

HS: It is difficult for you to understand why you would choose this while you are still here within the dream of separation. It was a choice made in ignorance of the outcome, while in a state of Perfection. Pain was unimaginable to you when you made this choice, and you did not know its outcome would be your suffering. It was an accident. A mistake. You've heard it defined as the "Original Sin." The Course however, defines sin differently than as you've been taught. In the Course, sin = separation or "error in thinking." In fact, you can use the two words interchangeably throughout the Course. You have the quote from the ACIM written down that describes the moment of your separation from Me. Please include that here now.

ME: Well, it's in among about one hundred pages of quotes I've collected from the Course. It's going to take some work for me to find it. If I'm really speaking to You, then shouldn't I be able to just receive it from You directly? Can't You just *give* me the exact quote? You know, just zap it into my head like you did for Helen?

HS: You would not be able to receive the words exactly as Helen scribed them. They would come out of you paraphrased, in your own version of My message.

ME: Why can't I receive them exactly as Helen herself heard them?

HS: Because you are not Helen. Every person who finds themselves in a body, will also automatically have an ego to go with it. No matter how spiritually advanced that person is, they will have an ego to deal with. It is through the filter of the ego that My words must pass, and every person's ego adapts them to the form most easily understandable to themselves. I took advantage of Helen's love of Shakespearian prose and iambic pentameter to create the *Course*. It is a timeless version of My Word. Timeless, in that as language evolves, it will remain understandable. There is no trace of the current vernacular in it.

ME: Interesting. Kind of like how most versions of the bible are filled with old words such as "thee" and "thou?" People don't actually talk like that anymore, and it sounds weird to us. The Course as scribed by

Helen will not become dated by its language like that?

HS: Correct. You, on the other hand, haven't got her type of mind. So when I speak to you, it comes out in your own vernacular.

ME: I see. Yeah, I have trouble even spelling iambic pentameter, much less writing an entire book in that style. I found that quote by the way. I now appreciate why You inspired me to gather all my favorite quotes, type them up, then correctly cite and place in order. I only had to search through about 100 pages of my own compilation, rather than 669 pages from the TEXT itself. Here is what it says about our "fall from grace":

The following quotation from the Course is from
TEXT Chapter 26 — V. The Little Hindrance
"The tiny instant you would keep and make eternal, passed away in Heaven too soon for anything to notice it had come. What disappeared too quickly to affect the simple knowledge of the Son of God can hardly still be there, for you to choose to be your teacher. Only in the past, - an ancient past, too short to make a world in answer to creation, - did this world appear to rise. So very long ago, for such a tiny interval of time, that not one note in Heaven's song was missed. Yet in each unforgiving act or thought, in every judgment and in all belief in sin, is that one instant still called back, as if it could be made again in time. You keep an ancient memory before your eyes. And he who lives in memories alone is unaware of where he is." (5:1-7)

ME: Okay, so how does this describe the moment we decided to give up our memory of You?

HS: The second you thought you could be something other than One with Me, you separated, and I immediately corrected that thought. You made an error in your judgment. You decided it was possible to be separate from Me, and My instantaneous correction for that thought was the reminder of your Oneness in God. The separation never truly happened. It is impossible to separate from Me. There was such a tiny interval between your thought of separation, and My Correction, "that not one note in Heaven's song was missed." In that

13

moment, the illusion of time and space was made; over seeming billions of years; as the something "other" than eternity. You now dream you left eternity, and moved into time. And here you appear to be stuck—coming back to this world again and again; keeping "an ancient memory before your eyes." You are completely unaware of your dreaming; reliving that moment of separation over millions of years, and seemingly living thousands of lifetimes. You're stuck in a time loop and don't know it. You can only step out of time and return to Me in eternity, through forgiving the unreality of this world you thought you made. You must choose to end your desire to be separate from Me and heal the illusion.

ME: How do I learn to do that?

HS: The lessons of the Course are designed to be one way in which you can wake up from the dream.

ME: Well alright then, let's keep moving forward. I want to do that!

Chapter 2: Lessons 6-10

Willingness To Forgive The Past

6. I am upset because I see something that is not there.

HS: The reality you're currently experiencing is extremely distressing. You go through your days in fear. Fear of what people think of you, fear of what they will say to you, and fear of what they've done or will do to you. In actuality, *what upsets you is not really there.* It's in the past. True reality is only found in the present moment.

7. I see only the past.

HS: Your minds carry the power of projection. You make what you see through your current thoughts. If you only have thoughts about the past, then the past will carry on into your future, showing you more of the same.

8. My mind is preoccupied with past thoughts.

HS: Your minds do not know how to let go of the past. You are preoccupied with past thoughts. You worry about what's already happened, and worry about future events based on the same sad past. You do not know how to fix this broken cycle, because you do not understand that you see nothing as it is in the present moment of now.

9. I see nothing as it is now.

HS: If you could witness all things as they truly exist in the present moment, and not as you see them with your past thoughts covering them, you would have no words to describe their heavenly beauty. Instead, you sit in the dark with the shades drawn, and wonder at your sorrows, not understanding why you suffer so.

10. My thoughts do not mean anything.

HS: Your thoughts have no meaning because they are based upon false data. Not a single thought that you have about the world is real, because it is based upon a world of illusion as it was seen in the past. Your mind is therefore actually blank, being preoccupied with nothing. Your only true thoughts, are the thoughts you think with God. These thoughts lie buried deep within you and it is these thoughts we are trying to uncover.

. . .

ME: I'm shocked to think my mind is actually blank, being filled with thoughts of the past. So You mean we're all walking around like mindless zombies? Attacking and hurting one another brainlessly? Ah-ha! I *knew* the zombie apocalypse was real! How do we stop this? What *are* the real thoughts we think with God? What kind of thoughts does God have?

HS: *You* are a Thought of God. Everyone is an individual Thought of God. You were each specifically thought of, and thus brought into being, by Him. This is why it feels so natural for you to call Him Father. You are all connected by His Love, having been Created by It. To share His Thoughts, is to share in His awareness of your Oneness in His Love. His Thoughts are an *experience of your Oneness.* The understanding of your Oneness would end all mindless harm towards one another instantly. You would see your fellow brothers as yourself, and would realize the senselessness of hurting them in any way. You'd see you were only hurting yourself alone.

ME: Oh, I see. Yeah, I can't say I have thoughts like that. How do I remember my real thoughts of Oneness with God and my fellow brothers then?

HS: Again, you forgive. You forgive the past in all you see- allowing all things to be as God Created them, not as you *think* they should be. Allow all things to be exactly as they are *now.* In the present moment. This includes people. *Especially* people. Then your mind is free from all you thought you were. You are then free to come Home to Me. This is a miracle.

The following quotations from the Course are from TEXT Chapter 28 — I. The Present Memory

"The miracle does nothing. All it does is to undo. And thus it cancels out the interference to what has been done." (1:1-3)

"The Holy Spirit can indeed make use of memory, for God Himself is there. Yet this is not a memory of past events, but only of a present state. You are so long accustomed to believe that memory holds only what is past, that it is hard for you to realize it is a skill that can remember *now*." (4:1-2)

"The Holy Spirit's use of memory is quite apart from time. He does not seek to use it as a means to keep the past, but rather as a way to let it go." (5:1-2)

"When ancient memories of hate appear, remember that their cause is gone. And so you cannot understand what they are for. (7:3-5)

"Be glad that it is gone, for this is what you would be pardoned from." (7:6)

"What *you* remember never was. It came from causelessness which you confused with cause." (9:1)

"When you forgive It for your sins, It will no longer be denied." (9:10)

"The miracle comes quietly into the mind that stops an instant and is still." (11:1)

"For in that instant does the Son of God do nothing that would make himself afraid." (12:6)

"What better way to close the little gap between illusions and reality than to allow the memory of God to flow across it, making it a bridge an instant will suffice to reach beyond?" (15:3)

"His Father wills that he be lifted up and gently carried over. He has built the bridge, and it is He Who will transport His Son across it. Have no fear that He will fail in what He wills. Nor that you can be excluded from the Will that is for you." (15:6-9)

ME: That sounds difficult. Impossible actually.

HS: For you alone, it *is* impossible. That is why I take this last step *with* each of you. I form the bridge over the final gap you must cross in your understanding of Who You Truly Are, and who you think you are now, as a body. All that's required from you, is just a small willingness to allow Me to do that.

ME: Oh, okay! I'm willing! Let's go!

HS: Hang on. Only I can see whether you are truly ready or not. You cannot just *say* it; it must be sincerely *felt and understood*. You have to *live* it. The key to this lies in truly understanding what it means to forgive. Once true forgiveness is understood and applied to your daily life, miracles begin to happen. You learn to live the truth of Who You Are, and miracles are a natural extension of that understanding. If you continue on with your thoughts as they are now, living in fear brought forward from the past, you will only see a future based on that fear. You will remain trapped here in the world of time. Thus making a senseless future exactly like the same senseless past. Your meaningless thoughts will continue to show you a meaningless world.

ME: I knew there was a catch. I suppose I have to go through all 365 lessons in order to fully understand our Oneness?

HS: No. You can fully understand your Oneness the moment you choose to. It's called the holy instant. These lessons only help remove the barriers you hold against such understanding.

ME: We'd better get back to the lessons then. My barriers to understanding are probably as big as mountains.

HS: Moving mountains is My specialty.

Chapter 3: Lessons 11-15

The True Power Of Our Thoughts

11. My meaningless thoughts are showing me a meaningless world.

HS: Your thoughts hold power. What you think, projects into your future. If you have thoughts based upon a past that is gone, you are having meaningless thoughts about nothing, which projects a meaningless world. On a level you are not aware, this is upsetting to you.

12. I am upset because I see a meaningless world.

HS: These thoughts you have about the past are manifesting insanity in your lives, and this is upsetting. You do not like what you see, and you feel powerless to change it. The world you see only increases your fear, reaffirming your already misguided thoughts.

13. A meaningless world engenders fear.

HS: The world you see is full of inconsistent happiness, pain, and misery at every turn. You cannot trust the world you live in to be kind to you; you cannot trust that the happiness it seems to bring will last. You are always living on the edge of fear, disaster, and pain. You feel that at any second, you could just lose everything that brings you any sense of joy.

14. God did not create a meaningless world.

HS: God is the One Constant. He is not chaos, fear or hate. He is only Love, and nothing but Love. And He cannot create anything that He is not. He [God] did not create the world you see. Your thoughts did.

15. My thoughts are images that I have made.

HS: The world God created is a world unlike any you can imagine. You cannot imagine it, because you do not remember the thoughts you think with God. You can be grateful that the world as you've made it here, is not real. The world you see now is made with the images of thoughts you had *alone*.

. . .

ME: Ok, let's address an issue I have. I have a hard time believing that all of us people made this world instead of God. I'm going to have a tough time accepting this idea. I was raised Catholic, with the idea that God (alone) created the world in seven days, blah blah blah.

HS: God is pure Love. There is nothing but Love within Him, and He cannot create what is unlike Himself. In fact, there *is* nothing else. *You* are made of His Perfect Love. This is the truth of Who You Are. God is incapable of creating a world of fear like the one you think you are in now. He did not make this mess. You did.

ME: Sigh. Why on earth would I make such a terrible place? I don't think I'd willingly choose to make something like this world. I don't believe You.

HS: Belief is not necessary in order for something to be true. You do not remember making this world, because this memory has been forgotten, along with your memory of Oneness. It is the nagging guilt of this long buried memory that causes all your grief. Yet, you only dream a dream that you separated from Me. No guilt should come into your mind over it, because it isn't true.

ME: I don't think I feel guilty for doing something I don't remember doing. I feel just fine in fact.

HS: Really? Why do you have times where sadness comes over you for no reason?

ME: I've always just blamed PMS.

HS: You would never feel angry, anxious, sad, depressed, or lonely again if you could but give up the underlying guilt that is causing it all. You only have one problem: your idea of separation from God. And there is only one solution: return to Him through forgiveness of this mistake in thought. There are quotes from the TEXT of the ACIM that support this idea. Please find them and include them here.

ME: Alright. Just so You know, I don't like paging through notes and finding quotes. It's tedious, time consuming, and frustrating.

HS: Yet you will still do this for Me. Thank you for your willingness to participate.

The following quotation from the Course is from
TEXT Chapter 6 — IV. The Only Answer

"Hear, then, the one answer of the Holy Spirit to all the questions the ego raises: You are a child of God, a priceless part of His Kingdom, which He created as part of Him. Nothing else exists and only this is real. You have chosen a sleep in which you have had bad dreams, but the sleep is not real and God calls you to awake." (6:1-3)

The following quotation from the Course is from
TEXT Chapter 8 — VI. The Treasure of God

"No one created by God can find joy in anything except the eternal; not because he is deprived of anything else, but because nothing else is worthy of him. What God and His Sons create is eternal, and in this and this only is Their joy." (3:2-3)

"We cannot be separated. Whom God has joined cannot be separated, and God has joined all His Sons with Himself. Can you be separated from your life and your being? The journey to God is merely the reawakening of the knowledge of where you are always, and what you are forever." (9:3-6)

HS: Your purpose here is simple, the journey short, and no sacrifice is being asked. All I am asking, is that you be willing to accept your Sonship with the Father and you will awaken in Him. Your "journey" to awakening will be over the holy instant that you do this.

ME: Yet it sounds like running a marathon. The act of running is simple in and of itself, but the overall task is extremely difficult.

HS: It can be, but only because you choose it to be so. As with running, with the proper mindset, it can be quite an enjoyable process.

ME: Hm. Right. I want to point out something here though. It seriously only took me about five seconds to find the above quotes. I literally just opened the document, and there they were! I couldn't believe how easy it was to find them!

HS: Soon, even *you* will believe in miracles.

ME: Well I still don't think it's possible to see another world other than the one I'm looking at right now. That miracle seems impossible.

HS: The way to Perfect Vision is just as simple as everything I will teach you. You need only remember that you are responsible for everything you see. All you need do is accept this and what you see will change.

The following quotations from the Course are from TEXT Chapter 21 — II. The Responsibility for Sight

"This is the only thing that you need do for vision, happiness, release from pain and the complete escape from sin, all to be given you. Say only this, but mean it with no reservations, for here the power of salvation lies:

> *I **am** responsible for what I see.*
> *I choose the feelings I experience, and I decide*
> *upon the goal I would achieve.*
> *And everything that seems to happen to me*
> *I ask for, and receive as I have asked.*

Deceive yourself no longer that you are helpless in the face of what is done to you. Acknowledge but that you have been mistaken, and all effects of your mistakes will disappear." (2:1-7)

"No accident or chance is possible within the universe as God created it, outside of which is nothing." (3:4)

"Be happy, and you gave the power of decision to Him Who

must decide for God for you. This is the little gift you offer to the Holy Spirit, and even this He gives to you to give yourself." (3:6-7)

Chapter 4: Lessons 16-20

Guilt, Suicide and Death

16. I have no neutral thoughts.

HS: You are always creating with the power of your thoughts, and you are always being guided by one of two teachers; only one of which is real. You are either using God as your guide for thinking, or the ego, which is nothing. Being nothing, the ego makes nothing. And each teacher will show you a different world. One that is real, and one that is nothing. You have no neutral thoughts and therefore see no neutral things.

17. I see no neutral things.

HS: What you see represents what you think. You see no neutral things, because all things stem from an inner choice you are perpetually making between God and the ego.

18. I am not alone in experiencing the effects of my seeing.

HS: You are never alone in experiencing the effects of how you choose to see the world. You are One, and as such, you experience your collective thoughts as One. You alone can change the world for everyone, by changing how you see it.

19. I am not alone in experiencing the effects of my thoughts.

HS: You are alone in nothing, because you're all held together by the same Grand Field of Unifying Energy: God's Love. God has a better world than this waiting for you. You can bring it here. Now. It's called "The Second Coming" by some. It is the *real* world, and you bring it about with your thoughts. Be determined to see it.

20. I am determined to see.

HS: You each share in the ability to shape your world with your thoughts, and if you want to see the real world, you must be determined to change how you see this one.

. . .

ME: Okay, so let me get this straight. You're saying that *You* didn't create the world we see. *We* did, through our decision to separate from You. You created a world much different from this one, which we refer to as Heaven, which is the place we left. We left it by mistake, because we didn't know that a fear based world like this one would arise from our decision to try and exist separate from You.

HS: Correct.

ME: And so we shouldn't blame *You* for this mess; we have only to blame ourselves?

HS: Correct.

ME: If all that's true, then I guess I can see where guilt and self blame would underly everything we see here.

HS: Do not blame yourself or anyone for anything. Nothing has happened. You are only dreaming that this has happened. I never threw you out of the Garden of Eden. And you never left. You just *think* you have. You have nothing to feel guilty about. Here I would like you to-

ME: I know, I know. Find the quote from the TEXT that talks about this. I'm way ahead of You.

HS: Great minds think alike.

ME: Ha ha. Very funny. I'm still not even sure You're real.

The following quotation from the Course is from TEXT Chapter 11 — IV. The Inheritance of God's Son

"The beginning phases of this reversal are often quite painful, as blame is withdrawn from without, there is a strong tendency to harbor it within. It is difficult at first to realize that this is exactly the same thing, for there is no distinction between within and without." (4:5-6)

**The following quotations from the Course are from
TEXT Chapter 11 — VIII. The Problem and the Answer**

"This is a very simple course. Perhaps you do not feel you need a course which, in the end, teaches that only reality is true. But do you believe it? When you perceive the real world, you will recognize that you did not believe it." (1:1-4)

"The end of the world is not its destruction, but its translation into Heaven." (1:8)

"You do not know the meaning of anything you perceive. Not one thought you hold is wholly true. The recognition of this is your firm beginning. You are not misguided; you have accepted no guide at all." (3:1-4)

"Yet your willingness to learn of Him depends on your willingness to question everything you learned of yourself, for you who learned amiss should not be your own teacher." (3:8)

"Ask, then, for what is yours, but which you did not make, and do not defend yourself against truth. You made the problem God has answered. Ask yourself, therefore, but one simple question:

Do I want the problem or do I want the answer?" (4:3-6)

HS: So whichever voice you decide to listen to, is the world you will see. Do you want to listen to your ego and remain here, or listen to Me, and see Heaven?

ME: Well I want to see Heaven of course, but how do I do this? If my thoughts about this world are all I know, and these thoughts all stem from the ego, and I will have an ego for as long as I'm in this body; then it sounds as if I have to die and leave my body in order to see Heaven. What am I supposed to do in order to hurry this along? Commit suicide?!?

HS: No. I am not advocating such a thing. You need not leave your body in order to experience the real world of Heaven.

ME: Oh. That makes me feel better. Just a quick question though. What *does* happen to suicides? Some people think they go to hell.

HS: There is no such thing as hell. I have set aside no special place of punishment, for no one is condemned. You are currently in as close an approximation to hell that there is. Hell is the idea of separation from Me, and this is the state you currently find yourselves in. While away from the body, you all return to the same place: My Love. While in the total and complete safety and comfort of My Love, you review your mistakes and accomplishments, you decide who will come with you on the next journey into the illusion, and it is here you practice loving without an ego. The ego dies with the body. It is not part of Who You Are, and you do not take it with you when your body dies.

ME: So does *anything* different happen to people who commit suicide?

HS: No, but I should explain that suicide is the route taken by a soul so deeply pained by this world; a soul so believing in the reality that they are a body; that they attempt to escape it by destroying themselves. It is the ultimate cry for Love. It is the ultimate attack upon the body. They feel so completely alone, abandoned, and separated that they simply cannot tolerate themselves any longer. They have completely forgotten the holiness and beauty of Who They Are. If this route is taken, it is not a shortcut out of the illusion, but rather only adds to the time it takes for release. Do not judge those who have destroyed their body in an attempt to escape this dream. In one past life or another, all of you have tried this means of escape, multiple times. Rejecting the body is not a solution. You will only have to come back here and try again to remember Who You Are. You will be gently guided in deciding to do this. Suicide is simply the longer road Home.

ME: I don't like to think that I have committed suicide in a past life. Eeek.

HS: Not all suicide is dramatic and obvious. Currently there is an epidemic of "suicidal behavior" on your planet right now. The desire for death is everywhere. You attempt to die in many ways. The most common and socially acceptable ways are those that involve addictions to food and chemicals. You do not love yourselves because you think the body is your identity, and so you abuse, neglect, and poison it in an effort to get rid of it. These behaviors are a choice for death, not life.

ME: I guess I never thought of it that way. So I can never have a beer or glass of wine again or You will look on me as wishing for death?

HS: No. You can still have those things. Just love yourself as you partake of them. Do not use them as an escape from your ego, the body, and its guilt.

ME: Oh, I can do that. Whew! And I'm relieved that this is as bad as it gets, and that there isn't any hell for anybody, and we're all treated with equal love when we die.

HS: You are correct. Suicide, and all other mistakes made within this dream are treated with equal love. You are all treated equally, because My love for you is equal. You each return to the realm of Spirit, but cannot stay permanently until all forms of sin (separation) are forgiven (let go). The world of separation must not tempt you to return in any way. All your business must be finished here; the obstacles to My peace must be overcome. Until then, your cycles of "birth" and "death" will go on.

ME: Okay, so how do we "finish our business here?" What are the obstacles to Your peace? Oh wait. That sounds vaguely familiar. I think I know what quote You're going to ask me to find. I'm starting to get into the swing of this You know. Somehow You're tricking me into enjoying this process of quote finding.

HS: I am tricking you into nothing. You've been tricking *yourself* for thousands of lifetimes. I'm just showing you how to uncover the truth and find peace. Finding peace feels enjoyable.

**The following quotations from the Course are from
TEXT Chapter 19 — IV. The Obstacles to Peace
C. The Third Obstacle: The Attraction of Death**

"And death is the result of the thought we call the ego, as

28

surely as life is the result of the Thought of God." (2:15)

"From the ego came sin and guilt and death, in opposition to life and innocence, and to the Will of God Himself." (3:1)

"One thing is sure; God, Who created neither sin nor death, wills not that you be bound by them." (3:3)

"The arrogance of sin, the pride of guilt, the sepulcher of separation, all are part of your unrecognized dedication to death." (4:5)

"You have another dedication that would keep the body incorruptible and perfect as long as it is useful for your holy purpose." (5:1)

"For God has answered this insane idea with His Own; an Answer which left Him not, and therefore brings thereafter to the awareness of every mind which heard His Answer and accepted It." (5:7)

"You who are dedicated to the incorruptible have been given through your acceptance, the power to release from corruption." (6:1)

"Those who fear death see not how often and how loudly they call to it, and bid it come to save them from communication." (7:1)

"Yet the retreat to death is not the end of conflict. Only God's Answer is its end." (7:3-4)

"My brother, child of our Father, this is a *dream* of death." (8:2)

"When anything seems to you to be a source of fear, when any situation strikes you with terror and makes your body tremble and the cold seat of fear comes over it, remember it is always for *one* reason; the ego has perceived it as a symbol of fear, a sign of sin and death." (11:1)

"Give it to Him to judge for you, and say:

Take this from me and look upon it, judging it for me.
Let me not see it as a sign of sin and death, nor use it for
destruction.
*Teach me how **not** to make of it an obstacle to peace, but let You use*
it for me, to facilitate its coming." (11:7-10)

HS: You only have to give up the *idea* you are a body, through looking upon it with forgiveness and lack of judgement; knowing it is not who you are. Your body doesn't have to *die*, in order for you to "rest in peace."

ME: I hope that wasn't meant to be funny. Anyway, I picked the third obstacle first; out of order from the other four. I picked it because it was about death. We somehow got sidetracked into talking about death.

HS: It doesn't matter what order we discuss them in. We will cover the other three obstacles to peace over the next three chapters.

Chapter 5: Lessons 21-25

The Fear Of God, Oneness, And More On Death

21. I am determined to see things differently.

HS: Your strife torn thoughts, have manifested a strife torn world. It is difficult to see beyond what your eyes behold, and so you must have a strong determination to look past it with forgiveness.

22. What I see is a form of vengeance.

HS: The world you see is your declaration of independence from God, and every form of separation it entails represents your vengeance against Him. There is only one way to escape the world you made and return to Heaven; you must give up these attack thoughts.

23. I can escape from this world by giving up attack thoughts.

HS: You must give up all thoughts of hatred and maliciousness towards your fellow brothers. You do this by forgiving their past. To truly forgive, is to look at your brothers as though you are seeing them for the first time. Do this for your own best interests; your own happy release from the illusion.

24. I do not perceive my own best interests.

HS: You have no idea who your brothers are in truth. How could you? You see each other as bodies. You do not perceive the world or your fellows correctly, and so you do now know what anything truly is or what it is for.

25. I do not know what anything is for.

HS: You do not know that everything exists for your own good; to learn to love, not hate. Everything is here for you to forgive.

. . .

ME: So if I cannot see anyone as they truly are, how do I learn to see them correctly? Every time I look at someone, I see their body, I hear the awful words they sometimes say, and I react as though all of it

31

is real. Because it *is* real to me! It seems impossible to see people any other way.

HS: This is because you *fear* to see them any other way. You fear them, because I am within them, and it is Me you are trying to avoid. It is actually *Me* you fear.

ME: I don't believe that. I seriously don't feel as though I'm trying to avoid You. I've spent my whole life praying to You, attempting to love You, find You, and understand You. How can You even *say* that I fear You?

HS: There is another obstacle you must overcome in order to get past your barriers to My peace. It lies buried deep within the inner recesses of your mind. So deep, the ego hopes you never discover it. To let go of this obstacle, would mean the undoing of your ego, and it does not want that. You have one fear, and one fear only: You are afraid of God.

ME: I don't feel afraid of You. I know you are kind, loving, and forgiving. I know there is no hell you would ever punish us with, and that You are waiting for us with open, loving arms. I know without a doubt that Your love is unconditional. Again, how can You say that I'm afraid of You?

HS: Because you attack your brothers in word, deed and thought. Attack anyone in any way, and you attack Me, for I am within them. Love them, and you love Me. To see them as part of yourself, is to see Me as part of yourself, and you will have accepted Me at last. You will have lost all fear of Me, no matter what form I may appear to you as. Then all your thoughts will be at peace towards yourself and everyone around you. You will have forgiven the world despite all the separation you see. Heaven will then come to replace this world, and your memory of Me will be restored.

ME: Oh. When you put it that way, I guess I still have some problems to work out. There are a few people out there who really irritate me sometimes. And some people I downright dislike. I don't feel ready to love *everyone* yet. It seems impossible to love *everyone*. Total love of everyone in the world is a long way off for me.

HS: It is not. Perhaps you should share the Fourth Obstacle to Peace now, and then we will discuss the times when you've achieved total love for everyone in the world. The moments when you were not afraid of Me; when you truly opened up and loved Me without your ego in the way.

The following quotations from the Course are from TEXT Chapter 19 — IV. The Obstacles to Peace
D. The Fourth Obstacle: The Fear of God

"Here is your promise never to allow union to call you out of separation; the great amnesia in which the memory of God seems quite forgotten; the cleavage of your Self from you; - *the fear of God*, the final step in your dissociation." (3:4)

"You are no more afraid of death than of the ego. These are your chosen friends. For in your secret alliance with them you have agreed never to let the fear of God be lifted, so you could look upon the face of Christ and join Him in His Father." (4:4-6)

"The desire to get rid of peace and drive the Holy Spirit from you fades in the presence of the quiet recognition that you love Him." (5:3)

"And now you stand in terror before what you swore never to look upon." (6:1)

"For you realize that if you look on this and let the veil be lifted, *they* will be gone forever. All of your "friends," your "protectors" and your "home" will vanish. Nothing that you remember now will you remember." (6:4-6)

"The Guide Who brought you here remains with you, and when you raise your eyes you will be ready to look on terror with no fear at all. But first, lift up your eyes and look on your brother in innocence born of complete forgiveness of his illusions, and through the eyes of faith that sees them not." (8:6-7)

"Here, with the journey's end before you, you see its purpose. And it is here you choose whether to look upon it or wander on, only to return and make the choice again." (10:7-8)

"To look upon the fear of God does need some preparation." (11:1)

"Before complete forgiveness you still stand unforgiving. You are afraid of God *because* you fear your brother. Those you do not forgive, you fear." (11:4-6)

"Beside you is one who offers you the chalice of Atonement, for the Holy Sprit is in him. Would you hold his sins against him, or accept his gift to you?" (13:1-2)

"Whom you forgive is free, and what you give you share. Forgive the sins your brother thinks he has committed, and all the guilt you think you see in him." (15:9-10)

"Free your brother here, as I freed you. Give him the selfsame gift, nor look upon him with condemnation of any kind." (18:1-2)

"Together we will disappear into the Presence beyond the veil, not to be lost but found; not to be seen but known." (19:1)

"Here is the rest and quiet that you seek, the reason for the journey from its beginning." (19:5)

HS: When you have learned to love Me within each of your brethren, you will have undone your fear of Me. You *have* achieved this a few times in your life, if only briefly.

ME: I think I know the moments You're talking about. There were three separate occasions in my life where I felt as though I'd slipped into Oneness with you. And I should share them now?

HS: Yes, please.

ME: Okay, I'll do my best to describe these three experiences. The first time I slipped into Oneness, I was only about twelve years old and had no idea what was happening to me. I was simply sitting on the couch one evening watching television with my family, when all of a sudden an overwhelming feeling of love welled up within my chest. It gradually increased in intensity and then began to spread outward through my arms and the top of my head. The level of love I was feeling was almost more than I could bear. I thought that perhaps I was dying. I also realized there was nothing I could do to stop this feeling. If I resisted it in any way, it only intensified. So I laid my head back on the couch and closed my eyes, wondering where this would go. I let it flow freely up and out through my upper body, and had the strange sensation of extending myself out into the world. I then became aware of my oneness with all living things; people, animals, plants; everything. The whole planet in fact! It was then that I became afraid. I thought I would extend so far out, that I wouldn't be able to come back. This single thought of fear ceased the feeling abruptly. I sat up and looked around the room and everything appeared perfectly normal. My family was all around, still watching television and talking. No one had any idea what had just happened to me. I didn't tell anyone either. I had no words to describe it, I didn't understand it, and I didn't want anyone trying to convince me it hadn't been a real experience.

I pondered this event many times over the course of the next few years, wondering what it meant. Until the second time it happened.

The second time came around about four years later, when I was about sixteen years old. We were driving back home to Minnesota from Boston Massachusetts after spending a few days moving my older brother James into pharmacy school there. I was sitting in the back seat, just staring out the window, when out of nowhere the same exact feeling of overwhelming love came over me once again.

As soon as I felt it, I thought, "Ok. I'm ready this time. I'm going to let this event go on as long as possible, because it's wonderful and I won't be afraid. I don't want it to end. I will keep my fear in check."

I laid my head back on the seat, closed my eyes, and let the feeling of love flood my body without any resistance from me.

Just as before, it began at the center of my chest and gently spread along my arms and out the top of my head. The feeling never went lower than my chest; it only spread upward and outward. I felt as though my heart was exploding with love. The intensity reached a point at which, once again, I had the vague sensation I might actually be dying. I laid there and went with it, trusting that this would not happen. From my single previous experience, I knew this amazing feeling would end if I became afraid.

Not only did I not die, but I became very much aware of life all around me. I allowed myself to become immersed in this oneness and felt a sense of joy so deep and so complete that I'm at a loss for words to describe it. I felt my soul blended with all living things at once, and yet, I did not lose my sense of "self identity." I could feel All Things and One Thing simultaneously. My individual personality remained intact, while my consciousness blended with infinity.

Then my mind went perfectly still and silent as I was suspended by the experience of total Oneness. An All Encompassing Love took over every sense. I did not hear or feel anything going on around me in the car, though I knew people were talking and the radio was playing. My bodily senses seemed to quit working altogether and I heard and felt only a deep silence.

I stayed there for a few moments, immersed in this profound sense of peace and love before the feeling began to gently recede of its own accord. I slowly came back to my normal bodily sensations and opened my eyes.

As before, no one in the car had any idea what had just happened to me and I didn't say a word about it.

There did not seem to be any trigger for these events. My life resumed to normalcy once again. I still had no idea what these experiences meant or what they were.

The third time I had this experience wasn't until about fourteen years later on September 12th, 2014. I know the date, because this event took place exactly one week after I began writing this book.

The night this event happened to me for the third time, my husband and I were sitting on the couch enjoying a rare movie night alone together; both kids were at sleepovers. So there I sat, totally engrossed in the movie, when that feeling of Total Love came over me. It was just as sublime as the previous two times, if not more intense. And just as before, once it peaked, it just gently faded away; the whole thing lasting only a few minutes at most.

However, at the end of this third experience, something different happened from the two previous times. I saw three orbs of bright light slightly off to my left, about fifteen feet away. Two were pure white and instantly disappeared when I looked directly at them. The third was a deep purple, which seemed to hesitate, then zoomed out of the room through the door. I didn't say a word to my husband. I just sat there as though nothing had happened. I never moved throughout the entire experience except to close my eyes while it took place. Again, I was too overwhelmed to share, nor could I put it into words at the time. Even here, I feel my words do no justice to these experiences.

HS: You experienced an example of what is referred to as the holy instant.

ME: It's nice to know what the experience is called, but I don't know how to live like that all the time. I mean, it's as though I have a split personality. The one that lives with You, and the one that lives here, in the illusion of separation.

HS: Until your mind is healed of the split between the ego and your Self, you *do* have a "split personality."

ME: How do I reach you directly like that on regular basis? I'd love to feel One with You all the time.

The following quotations from the Course are from MANUAL FOR TEACHERS 26. Can God Be Reached Directly?

"God indeed can be reached directly, for there is no distance between Him and His Son. His awareness is in everyone's memory, and His Word is written on everyone's heart. Yet this awareness and this memory can arise across the threshold of recognition only where all barriers to truth have been removed." (1:1-3)

"Sometimes a teacher of God may have a brief experience of direct union with God. In this world, it is almost impossible that this endure." (3:1-2)

"If it happens, so be it. If it does not happen, so be it as well. All worldly states must be illusory. If God were reached directly in sustained awareness, the body would not be long maintained." (3:5-8)

HS: *You* do nothing of yourself. There is nothing you can do to induce such a state. It comes from Me, and I bring it to you once your barriers to Me have been removed. And even then, you may not have such an experience until the moment of your physical death. Such a state cannot be maintained by the body. It is too dense to contain My Light. The reason you had those three experiences, was due to forgiveness lessons that you accomplished in your future. Healing in the future, came back to bring you healing in the past.

ME: Wait, *what*? Say that again please? Using words I can understand? If that's even possible?

HS: Time and eternity cannot be reconciled. They are distinct, separate states. Your Self, which dwells with Me, exists only in eternity, where nothing has ever happened to you to change Who You Are. The person you know yourself to be here in time, in a body, having linear experiences in time, can be affected at any moment by your One Self- Who knows no time. Events seem to happen to you in the past or future, but in reality everything exists only in the eternal moment of *now*.

ME: Um. Right. Sorry. I just can't wrap my head around it. I do have a different question though. What were those orbs of light I saw at the end?

HS: They were a *Who*, not a *what*. They were dear ancient friends of yours. You could see them momentarily because you stepped out of time into eternity. You briefly moved out of your body, and into the realm of Spirit.

ME: I moved out of my body and into the realm of Spirit? That sounds like death. Are You saying that I *died*?!

HS: If what you call a shift in awareness from your body to Spirit "death," then yes, you died. Only momentarily though.

ME: Give me a minute here. I need to process this.

(At this point I racked my memory of these events, trying to discern exactly when I'd felt as though I'd actually "died." I couldn't determine an exact moment.)

ME: So that was death? Why, that felt like no change at all! I simply went from feeling ordinary, to extraordinary.

HS: Precisely. Death of the body is no change at all because it's not Who You Are. Leaving it behind is no big deal. Death as you think of it, is really a simple shift in awareness from the body to Spirit. It is the gentlest experience you will ever have in contrast to the one you're having now. There is nothing to fear about death. Only the ego fears death of the body, because only the ego stands to be lost along with it.

The following quotations from the Course are from TEXT Chapter 18 — VI. Beyond the Body

"There is nothing outside you. That is what you must ultimately learn, for it is the realization that the Kingdom of Heaven is restored to you." (1:1-2)

"The body is outside you, and but seems to surround you,

39

shutting you off from others and keeping you apart from them, and them from you. It is not there. There is no barrier between God and His Son, nor can His Son be separated from Himself except in illusions. This is not his reality, though he believes it is." (9:1-4)

"You cannot put a barrier around yourself, because God placed none between Himself and you." (9:10)

"Everyone has experienced what he would call a sense of being transported beyond himself. This feeling of liberation far exceeds the dream of freedom sometimes hoped for in special relationships. It is a sense of actual escape from limitations." (11:1-3)

"You have escaped from fear to peace, asking no questions of reality, but merely accepting it. You have accepted this instead of the body, and have let yourself be one with something beyond it, simply by not letting your mind be limited by it." (11:10-11)

"This can occur regardless of the physical distance that seems to be between you and what you join; of your respective positions in space; and of your differences in size and seeming quality." (12:1)

"There is no violence at all in this escape. The body is not attacked, but simply properly perceived." (13:1-2)

"In these instants of release from physical restrictions, you experience much of what happens in the holy instant; the lifting of the barriers of time and space, the sudden experience of peace and joy, and, above all, the lack of awareness of the body, and of the questioning whether or not all this is possible." (13:6)

"It is possible because you want it. The sudden expansion of awareness that takes place with your desire for it is the irresistible appeal the holy instant holds." (14:1-2)

ME: Well if that expansion of my awareness was "death" or what You're referring to as the holy instant, then where was Heaven? You know, the tunnel and all that?

HS: I did not assist you with the next step, because you are not ready for that yet. You have more to do here before you will desire to fully let your body go. Then I will carry you across the final gap to Heaven.

ME: So I just got a brief taste of the initial step of what it's like to leave my body, "die" and experience Oneness?

HS: Correct.

ME: Will I ever see those orbs of light again? My ancient friends I mean?

HS: They are with you now. They are with you always. They are part of your One Self, Whose eyes you used to see them.

Chapter 6: Lessons 26-30

Our Belief The Body Is Who We Are

26. My attack thoughts are attacking my invulnerability

HS: Nothing in all the universe can harm you. You are completely invulnerable. Yet the world you experience is one of loss, despair, and fleeting happiness, which makes it seem as though you must maintain a near constant state of either attack or defense. This state of mind blocks your inner eyes from My World.

27. Above all else I want to see.

HS: You have forgotten that you're invulnerable, and so you see yourself as susceptible to attack. You must learn to see yourself as the unassailable Holy Son of God that you truly are, if you want to see Me in all things.

28. Above all else I want to see differently.

HS: Deep down, above all else, you want to see Me. To do this, you must look at all things differently.

29. God is in everything I see.

HS: It is Me you are trying to see in all things. To do this, you need to look beyond what your body's eyes show you with total faith and love that I am there.

30. God is in everything I see because God is in my mind.

HS: Where should you look for Me? I am here. Within you. Therefore you cannot see Me outside yourself; you must use your eyes that lie within.

. . .

ME: So, to sum this up, we need to see past each other's bodies in order to become aware our minds are connected to God. That's a tall order. We judge one another all the time based on what we see. This is how we categorize each other, summarize what we think we know, and then judge based on the "facts" we've gathered. How do we change this?

HS: This is actually addressed in the second obstacle to My peace. You have to let go of the idea that you are a body all together. You have to give up the idea that the body will bring you happiness.

ME: Let me guess. Now would be a good time to insert that quote from the TEXT?

HS: Correct.

The following quotations from the Course are from TEXT Chapter 19 — IV. The Obstacles to Peace B. The Second Obstacle: The Belief the Body is Valuable for What It Offers

"What has the body really given you that justifies your strange belief that in it lies salvation? Do you not see that this is the belief in death?" (2:6-7)

"Here is the source of the idea that love is fear." (2:9)

"It is only the messengers of fear that see the body, for they look for what can suffer. Is it a sacrifice to be removed from what can suffer?" (3:3-4)

"Forgive me all the sins you think the Son of God committed. And in the light of your forgiveness he will remember who he is, and forget what never was." (6:2-3)

"Forgive me your illusions, and release me from punishment for what I have not done." (8:1)

"I am within your holy relationship, yet you would imprison me behind the obstacles you raise to freedom, and bar my way to you." (8:3)

"It is impossible to seek for pleasure through the body and not find pain. It is essential that this relationship be understood, for it is one the ego sees as proof of sin." (12:1-2)

"The attraction of guilt *must* enter with it, and whatever fear

43

directs the body to do is therefore painful. It will share the pain of all illusions, and the illusion of pleasure will be the same as pain." (12:6-7)

"To you it teaches that the body's pleasure is happiness. Yet to itself it whispers, "It is death." (13:7-8)

"Not one but must regard the body as himself, without which he would die, and yet within which is his death equally inevitable." (6:5)

HS: Do you see the double-edged sword belief in yourself as a body is? You think you will die without your body, yet its death is inevitable. Death begins at birth. The body can bring you nothing but pain, sadness, and suffering, and yet you cling to it with your last dying breath.

ME: Yeah, but isn't it good to want to stay alive?

HS: It isn't the desire to *live* you must give up, but rather, the idea that the body is your identity. It does not matter what form you've chosen to appear in this dream as; you can be any race, color, gender or sexual orientation. None of it matters, because it is not Who You Are. Give up all the mistaken identities you've taken on, and know beneath it all, you are each an equal part of My holy Sonship.

ME: Give up all our identities? That sounds tough. Some people make a big deal over the identities of themselves in comparison to others; thinking they're better or more superior to others. For instance, there are those who don't like gay people, and some are against certain races, religions, and genders. And some people really get riled up over foreigners. The list of ways we've found to see differences and dislike one another seems endless. In fact, some people claim that they've found bible passages that support their reasons for hating others. They claim these are words You've said Yourself. For example, some say that You're against people being gay, and that women are not equal to men. Heaven help a gay woman I guess. And please don't make me find those bible quotes. I can't bring myself to do that.

HS: No, I won't make you find those bible quotes, because those particular quotes are not My words. Not all the words in the bible are Mine.

ME: Well, there are people out there who say You would never allow untruths to be written in the bible. Some say every single word of it is true. I don't believe this, but if the truth can't be trusted to be found in the bible, then how can we trust *any* book to be a source of spiritual truth?

HS: Dear child, know this, and know it well. My Word is not found outside of you. My Word can only be found within. *I have written My Word within the heart of every human being.* That is where truth is found. You will never find Me outside your Self, though words can be used to lead you to Me within.

ME: Well then is *any* of the bible true?

HS: Yes, of course there is much truth written in it.

ME: Well, which parts? How do we know which words are true, and which ones aren't?

HS: The only words in the bible that are truth are the loving ones. You must weigh the words you read; against the love you feel when you read them. If the words you read inspire love and peace within your heart, My messenger speaks the truth. I am Love, and speak only the language of Love. If you still have doubts, simply ask yourself if the message brings people together, or separates them? Do the words promote conflict, or inspire peace? If they do not encourage good works and kindness towards your fellows, they are not Mine. Only the ego engenders fear, conflict and separation. Only the ego sees differences and would encourage lovelessness. Use the feeling in your heart as the judge of truth in anything you read.

ME: Ahhhhhh, so we should read everything with our bullshit meter on. How did Your words get intertwined with the words of the ego in the first place? Why *would* You allow that?

HS: Do you think the motives of the ego have changed over the eons? Do you think I would forcefully intervene back then, any more than now? I will not force My Will upon your hearts. You must come to Me willingly. You were as free to speak and write then, as you are now. Not only that, but the people who taught what you now find in the bible, had no idea 2000 years ago that it would be compiled into a book that would serve as the backbone of a major religion.

ME: Would the apostles have written it differently if they had?

HS: No. First, they did not write the bible. Second, they did not have the resources of today with which to spread the Good News, and had to painstakingly deliver it in person, traveling long distances on foot from place to place. This took up much of their time. Though inefficient, it was still the best way to share information, because the populace was largely illiterate at the time. The bible was compiled later on by others- alongside their own ego agendas.

ME: Why didn't You just give us *A Course in Miracles* back then, instead of the bible?

HS: Jesus gave His message in its most simple form: Love one another as He loves you. It can also be worded: Do unto others, as you'd have done to you. And the shortest version of all: Be kind. This was the most drastic religious change the people could accept at the time. A book like the Course would not have been practical. It would've been like introducing algebra to a child just learning addition. The spiritual jump forward would've been too great. The bible was a necessary intermediary step in your spiritual progression. It has served a good purpose. Do not assume I am displeased the ego has crept into it. I am not. Nothing that happens within the illusion could displease Me. There is nothing any of you could ever do to displease Me. Everything is happening according to My plan.

ME: So I guess the bible really helped us then, despite its faults.

HS: You have no idea. Be grateful for what the bible has brought humanity, as well as *all other books and teachings* that contain My Word of peace. My Word is written in many ways, in many forms. You have studied the bible and other peaceful teachings during your many past lives and this has brought you to where you are now.

ME: You say "many past lives." How long have I been at this? How many past lives have I lived?

HS: You have visited this illusion exactly 5,712 times.

ME: Holy moly. That's a lot. I must be some special kind of stupid.

HS: Actually, you're doing quite well. It takes an average of about 10,000 lifetimes to awaken.

ME: No wonder we all feel so exhausted.

HS: That's why you are writing these words. Everyone is tired of the ego and tired of coming here, but most of them cannot see the way out. Books like the Course, and many others are being written to save people countless pointless journeys here.

ME: So what is the next step in Your Plan?

HS: My Plan now, is to present the teachings of Jesus once again, in as simple a form as possible, so that you may learn to *live* them. The most complete compilation so far is *A Course in Miracles*. It is time to learn how to *apply* and *live* My truth. That is why God's truth is called the Living Word of God. It is truly alive, and It's about to have a growth spurt.

ME: I'm awed by all this information. I've never considered any of these things before this conversation. You're pretty smart, you know that? Where were You when I was taking algebra and physics? Not to mention my college pharmacy classes?

HS: Who do you think gave you the perseverance?

ME: Oh, good point. I'm guessing You've helped me through countless situations, while all along I've thought I've done it all by myself; giving no credit or gratitude to You.

HS: A good parent does not help their child expecting gratitude or appreciation in return. A good parent helps their child out of love, and expects nothing in return.

ME: Well this child is going to do her utmost to remember she's not alone in anything she does. And to try to see You in every person, instead of the body.

Chapter 7: Lessons 31-35

World Peace

31. I am not the victim of the world I see.

HS: You are victim to nothing, because you are the decider of all you see and experience. You can set down your burdens, and come down from your cross at anytime. You have invented all you see.

32. I have invented the world I see.

HS: You can decide there is another way of looking at the world. You can decide to see peace instead of conflict. Peace is what holds My Unified Field of Love together. Peace is what lies behind this world of solid matter. Seeing My peace behind all things is the new way you must learn to look at the world.

33. There is another way of looking at the world.

HS: Everything you see would literally fall to pieces without My peace. All the molecules in the universe are held together in peaceful cooperation and harmony through the Unity they share in My peace. When things seem to fall apart, remember to choose to see peace instead.

34. I could see peace instead of this.

HS: Choose to see My loving peace behind all things, despite the conflict and separation your eyes may show you. You can do this, because your mind is part of Mine. You are very holy.

35. My mind is part of God's. I am very holy.

HS: You cannot be at One with something, and be at war with it at the same time. You are either at peace, or you are at odds. Your mind cannot serve two masters. In truth, you abide in God, and He is the only Master. You share Unity with His Mind, because you are created from Him. All living things are very holy, being wholly part of God.

. . .

ME: Interesting that all matter would simply fall apart if molecules didn't cooperate peacefully. Is that why the world we see is full of conflict and chaos? Because we refuse to cooperate? The world is falling apart, because we're choosing to *be* apart?

HS: Correct. You are actively resisting your natural state of Oneness, by refusing to accept peace.

ME: I don't feel as though I'm actively resisting peace. I *want* peace! And I think a lot of other people do too. How are we actively resisting peace?

HS: Now I would like you to quote the first obstacle to My peace, and then we will discuss how to correct it on a global level.

**The following quotations from the Course are from
TEXT Chapter 19 — IV. The Obstacles to Peace
A. The First Obstacle: The Desire to Get Rid of It**

"Would you let a little grain of sand, a wall of dust, a tiny seeming barrier, stand between your brothers and salvation? And yet, this little remnant of attack you cherish still against your brother *is* the first obstacle the peace in you encounters in its going forth." (2:9-10)

"You still oppose the Will of God, just by a little. And that little is a limit you would place upon the whole." (3:3-4)

"Peace could no more depart from you than from God. Fear not this little obstacle." (4:3-4)

"The little wall will fall away so quietly beneath the signs of peace." (4:11)

"For in the miracle of your holy relationship, without this barrier, is every miracle contained." (5:2-4)

"No illusions stand between you and your brother now." (6:3)

"This feather of a wish, this tiny illusion, this microscopic remnant of the belief in sin, is all that remains of what once seemed to be the world. It is no longer an unrelenting barrier to peace." (8:1-2)

"I am made welcome in the state of grace, which means you have at last forgiven me." (17:1)

"Salvation is looked upon as a way by which the Son of God was killed instead of you. Yet would I offer you my body, you whom I love, *knowing* its littleness? Or would I teach that bodies cannot keep us apart?" (17:4-6)

ME: So the very first obstacle to peace, is the fact that we see each other as bodies, which is to see sin, which is another name for the error of our separation. The body is the barrier we have placed between ourselves and You. Correct?

HS: Correct.

ME: You said we would talk about how to overcome this obstacle on a global level next. Are you talking about world peace?

HS: Yes.

ME: Alright. Lay it on me. I'm not holding my breath here, because people have been trying to come up with a plan for world peace for a long time. I find it hard to believe You will give me any real answers.

HS: Have faith in Me. I will not disappoint you. You already know that part of achieving world peace entails people finding their own inner peace. This is the peace of knowing your brother is One with you. The body must not be seen as a boundary between you. The next step then, is to extend this thought to the world, and see no boundaries between lands, nations and cultures. This transformation is achieved through a new, unified world government. All boundaries between countries must be eliminated and the world joined together as one land and people.

ME: Whoa whoa whoa. I've never been a fan of the idea of world domination. Is that what You're talking about here? *That's* Your plan for world peace? Uh nope. None for me thanks.

HS: Please listen carefully. The new world government would be arranged as such: One world ruler, who holds no real power except as the spokesperson for a group of twelve, who each oversee one of the twelve basic human needs. Every human being in the world has the same basic needs, no matter where they live, who they are, or what culture they come from. If these needs were equally met among all peoples, there would be no strife, no trying to overcome, and no desire to move somewhere else where "things might be better."

ME: I'm still not sold on this idea. It sounds like communism or an evil dictatorship waiting to happen.

HS: Actually, this is the same social dynamic Jesus set up with His twelve apostles. Each had a single responsibility to fulfill for the group, be it procuring money, food, shelter, leisure activities etc. In this way, they took care of each other. It ran flawlessly.

The twelve basic (non spiritual) human needs are (listed in order of urgency):

1. Food
2. Clothing
3. Shelter
4. Health Care
5. Finances
6. Transportation
7. Global Relations
8. Education
9. Environment
10. Personal Liberties
11. Crime
12. Leisure

ME: I'm surprised "global relations" is higher than "education." Why is that?

HS: Believe Me, if you were raising your children in a war torn third world country, societal peace would be more important to you than putting their lives at risk just to send them to school.

ME: Understood. And by "Crime" You mean the control of it and everything that entails?

HS: Yes.

ME: I still have a problem with all this. Thirteen people running the entire world seems like too much power in the hands of too few. There's still too much opportunity for corruption. No thanks.

HS: Let Me continue to explain. These twelve people would each have twelve more people beneath each of them, and those twelve would each have twelve, and so on and so forth, extending outward until this pattern reached all the way down to the local community level. Imagine it arranged as concentric, interlocking rings, uniformly covering the globe.

ME: That sounds confusing, but it's a much better distribution of power. So how many people would end up being in this "New World Government" once it's all said and done?

HS: 144,000.

ME: (After a moment of stunned silence.) Are we talking about *the* 144,000? As in the biblical reference to this number?

HS: Yes. The very one.

ME: I don't know much about this number, except I've heard that some people ridiculously interpret this bible passage to mean that there are only 144,000 of God's "chosen ones," who will end up being "saved" and allowed to go to Heaven.

HS: That passage has been greatly misunderstood. I have not chosen 144,000 people that will be saved *from* the world, but rather, I have asked for 144,000 volunteers *to save the world*. There's a big difference in meaning.

ME: I think I'd actually like to take a look at that bible chapter if You don't mind? I have no idea what it actually says about all this. Would

You like me to include it, so that others may read it for themselves as well?

HS: Yes, it would please Me very much if you did that.

ME: Let the pleasing begin then.

This was a vision experienced by the apostle John:

"After this I saw four angels standing at the four corners of the earth, holding back its four winds so that no wind would blow on land or sea or on any tree. And I saw another angel ascending from the east, with the seal of the living God. And he called out in a loud voice to the four angels who had been given power to harm the land and the sea: "Do not harm the land or sea or trees until we have sealed the foreheads of the servants of our God."

And I heard the number of those who were sealed, one hundred forty-four thousand from all the tribes of Israel:

(Here the bible lists each of the twelve tribes of Israel.)

After this I looked and saw a multitude too large to count, from every nation and tribe and people and tongue, standing before the throne and before the Lamb. They were clothed in white robes, with palm branches in their hands. And they cried out in a loud voice:

"Salvation to our God, who sits on the throne, and to the Lamb!"

And all the angels stood around the throne and around the elders and the four living creatures. And they fell facedown before the throne and worshiped God, saying, "Amen! Blessing and glory and wisdom and thanks and honor and power and strength to our God forever and ever! Amen."

Then one of the elders addressed ME: "These in white

robes," he asked, "who are they, and where have they come from?"

"Sir," I answered, "you know."

So he replied, "These are the ones who have come out of great tribulation; they have washed their robes and made them white in the blood of the Lamb. For this reason,

'They are before the throne of God and serve Him day and night in His temple; and the One seated on the throne will spread His tabernacle over them. Never again will they hunger, and never will they thirst; nor will the sun beat upon them, nor any scorching heat. For the Lamb in the center of the throne will be their shepherd. He will lead them to fountains of living water, and God will wipe every tear from their eyes.'" (Holy Bible, King James Version, Revelations 7)

HS: Every boundary around every country will have to come down in order for a world government to work. People will have to learn to see themselves as a global community; everyone as on the same side. The "angel of the east" represents China and India- the first two countries to dissolve the boundary between themselves. This is referenced in Revelations by, "And I saw another angel ascending in the east..." The other four angels "who had been given power to harm the land and the sea..." represent the other four most powerful countries holding nuclear capabilities: the United States, Russia, United Kingdom and France. China and India will set the example for the other four countries to join with them into one government, "calling out in a loud voice," and the rest of the world- not wanting to be left out- will quickly follow suit.

ME: What precipitates the downfall of the boundary between China and India? Why do they do that?

HS: It is triggered by an unfortunate and unforeseen combination of social, economic and environmental hardships and catastrophes. They simply *must* join together in order for their peoples to survive. But out of the ashes of despair, a new system of self-government arises; driven forward by the people themselves. They will choose not to reestablish their old way of being. And what they come up with, will astound the world. The speed of their recovery from near devastating cataclysm will appear nothing short of miraculous.

ME: Oh my goodness! So who are the 144,000 then?

HS: They are the souls around the world who currently are, have, and will, become enlightened through learning My message of peace contained in *A Course in Miracles* and other similar works. They will incarnate together, spanning across three generations; a mixture of the old and young. They are My peacekeepers; My servants who will assist in the great world change from one of fear, to one of love. They will come from every corner of the world, forming the first 144,000 members of the new world government. Never in the history of this planet, will so many enlightened souls have incarnated together. Never in the history of the planet, will so many peacekeepers have come. In My peace, lies their strength.

ME: This reminds me of another quote from the Course: "This is what is meant by 'the meek shall inherit the earth.' They will literally take it over because of their strength." (ACIM T. Chapter 2.II.7:4-5)

HS: Yes, that is what I'm referring to. After each of them leaves the planet at the end of their lives, those who take their place will only gain those positions through demonstrating their humanitarian capabilities; their capacity for selflessness, compassionate human understanding, wisdom, ethics, and a deep love for humankind. There will be no more political parties; no more division. You will all agree you have the same basic human needs, and that you must work together to meet them. All boundaries seen between all nations will fall. This is how the first obstacle to peace will be overcome on a global level, as people reach out towards one another in love, helpfulness and human kindness.

ME: Wow. Okay, so we have 144,000 enlightened peace loving people overseeing the twelve basic physical human needs of the world. Who pays for all this? Are we taxed 95% or something? I'm still not ruling out communism.

HS: Please take careful note: You will not be *under any* government at all per se. You will be cooperating together in a global *self* government. You will be under no rulership but your own.

ME: Oh, got it. No evil dictatorship and no communism. We're taking care of ourselves, that's all.

HS: Correct. Now back to your question about taxation. Actually, only 24% will be taken from each person's personal earnings to fund these needs. There will be no taxation beyond this. The first 12% will go to the local community of each individual, and the other 12% will go into the global collection. One percent will be given to each of the twelve areas of need in each case.

ME: So there will be no individual countries, no health insurance, no starvation and no political parties?

HS: Correct. But there *will* be a single world currency, a single world language, and let's not forget: World peace.

ME: That sounds awesome. But I still don't see how everyone just giving 24% of their income will take care of all the world's needs. Are You sure that's enough money to go around? I mean, is everything just...free?

HS: No, everything will not be free. You would still pay for what you want above and beyond the basics. For instance, if you needed a home, a basic one would be provided, but if you wanted something more extravagant, then it would be paid for out of your own pocket. If you were unable to work, or refused to work, you would be provided with food, clothing, shelter, healthcare and access to public transportation. No money would be given, but rather, only the actual goods themselves. All the basic needs of every person would be met. If you desired more than that, you would have to pay for it. If you wanted to go to school to get a better job and earn more money, you could attend any level of education at no cost. Your only limit would be your own willingness.

ME: Oh, so all people would just receive the basics to survive. Even so, are You sure there'd be enough money to pay for all that?

HS: People in your country raise millions of dollars in just a few weeks through your ticket lotteries. Lotteries, where only a few dollars are spent per person, by only *part* of the population; most do not spend even close to 24% of their income. Now imagine if all the people of the world donated greater to their own sustainability? Yes, there is plenty to take care of yourselves. The new system will be fluid and dynamic; currency from one area can be transferred to another if there is temporarily a greater social need. And the cost of living will be greatly reduced. You'd be surprised at how affordable things become when all greed and corruption is removed from the system.

ME: This all makes sense, and at the same time, sounds as impossible as me loving everyone on the planet. I have another question though. I thought You said this world was all a dream? Why are we bothering to "save" a dream? Don't we just want to go Home to You and live in the real world of Heaven? Why waste any time improving *this* place?

HS: Because there are many who must still return here to learn their lessons in love and forgiveness. These lessons are learned more quickly in a peaceful, loving environment. Everyone's spiritual growth will be greatly accelerated after these global changes. This nightmare can only shift into a happy dream through your own willingness to change it.

ME: Ah, as quoted in the ACIM: "This world will change through you. No other means can save it, for God's plan is simply this: The Son of God is free to save himself, given the Word of God to be his Guide, forever in his mind and at his side to lead him surely to his Father's house by only love." (WORKBOOK Lesson 125.2:1-2)

HS: Correct. You do this by dismantling all boundaries within your mind. See nobody as a separate body, and no country as a separate place from where you live. Everyone is living on this planet, in this dream, together.

ME: Will any of this happen in my lifetime?

HS: No. Your children's children will see the first implementation of this system during their aged years. Their children will then live under the benevolent leadership of this new world government. You will leave this planet just as the idea is beginning to form a bud- not yet ready to blossom. It will take a generation of time to work out the details.

ME: So it will happen in roughly 200 to 300 years? That seems kind of far away, but at least we don't blow ourselves up. Will I come back among the 144,000?

HS: No. This will be your last trip into the illusion.

ME: Normally, hearing that would make me feel ecstatic, but I'm disappointed I'm not coming back to live during this spiritually exciting time.

HS: You're already living during a spiritually exciting time. Look at what you're doing right now.

ME: I suppose so. Do I know anyone in this life who will be coming back to be among the 144,000?

HS: You know some of them. Many of whom will one day hold this book in their hands.

ME: That's awesome. I can't wait to tell all my family and friends they're going to be among the 144,000 peace bringers in their next life!

HS: Keep in mind they are not being singled out as special. They are simply the ones who volunteered for this particular role in bringing peace to the world. *Everyone* is tasked with bringing peace to this illusion through his or her individual choice to remember My love and holiness envelops all they see.

Chapter 8: Lessons 36-40

Intergalactic Peace snd Aliens

36. My holiness envelops everything I see.

HS: Looking at the world through eyes of Oneness and shared holiness will bring nothing but peace forward from the Field of Unity. You will realize it is not only *you* that is blessed by your holiness, but that your holiness *blesses the world*. You are all enveloped by a shared holiness.

37. My holiness blesses the world.

HS: God's Life Force is everywhere, in everything, and you are all a part of it. You bless the world with your holiness, because you are part of All That Is. And there is nothing your holiness cannot do.

38. There is nothing my holiness cannot do.

HS: This power is so unlimited, so vast and all encompassing, that there is nothing it cannot do, and no part of this illusion it cannot heal.

39. My holiness is my salvation.

HS: There is nothing greater than the power of your holiness, and you all share in it. Your holiness salvages you from everything you fear through realizing this truth.

40. I am blessed as a Son of God.

HS: Rather than seeing loss and depravation all around you, know that you are a blessed part of My Sonship, and you already *have* and *are* everything. The world can never give you this blessing, but I have.

. . .

ME: Okay, I understand we are all connected by Your Power and share in Your abilities. I understand we can open up to Your Power through aligning ourselves with Your Will; Your Oneness. This is done by seeing our Oneness in everyone else, because You are in them, and we are in

You. This still sounds like a lot of impossible work, but I'll believe it can happen anyway. Let's fast forward now to when we have achieved world peace. What then?

HS: Once you have achieved world peace, the next boundary will fall; the boundary between your planet and the rest of the living universe. You will receive open contact from those who have been waiting for your spiritual evolution; those who are here with you in the illusion, in other bodies, on other inhabited worlds.

ME: Wait just one minute. Do You mean *alien contact*?

HS: If you are referring to other sentient life forms, from other galaxies as "aliens," then yes, I mean alien contact. They will make full contact once you have achieved a level of peace and love that matches theirs.

ME: Why do we have to wait until we've achieved their level of love and peace? Why can't they just come help us now?

HS: Because your current level of fear is far too great. They literally cannot make it through the barrier of fear surrounding this planet. The frequencies have to match. Love can only merge with Love.

ME: What about all those people claiming to have had alien abductions? I'm not sure I've ever been abducted, but I've seen some weird stuff. Are all those stories fabricated? And what about crop circles?

HS: Some of what you speak of, your own people have done to one another; while the rest has truly has been done by those who live on other "nearby" planets. There are a total of 36 planets in your same predicament. You are all temporarily quarantined by your own fear. Earth is the worst of them; hence the reason why Jesus chose your planet out of all the inhabited worlds in the Grand Universe to come to. You need the most help and His teachings of peace would have the greatest impact- the greatest contrast to the rest of the living universe. Yours is not the only planet benefiting from His teachings. An entire superuniverse learns from our Creator Son as they watch the story of your planet unfold.

ME: So are there other unloving beings out there? Those who want to take over the earth and mutilate us? Please just tell me everything!

HS: I will keep this as brief as possible, because we will deal with this at length in your next book. I don't wish to deviate too far from learning the Workbook lessons from the Course, which are My main focus here.

ME: Got it. I will contain my questions as best I can. Please go on.

HS: Of the 36 planets quarantined by fear, only three have achieved the ability to reach you. At the time, they were more spiritually evolved, but not by much. They could reach you, only because they vibrated to a similar frequency and had the technology. Over the past two decades, they have gradually lost the ability to reach your frequency, because they made a spiritual leap; which has temporarily cut them off from you, until you catch up. They no longer seek your genetics, nor have any other reason to bring you aboard their ships. They are now wholly peaceful and loving, whose gentle planets are at the point yours will be in the next 200 to 300 years. They are on the cusp of spiritual integration with the rest of the living universe. There is now no place in the grand universe as difficult to live on as earth. Count yourselves among the bravest of the brave, the most ambitious, and the most courageous souls- just for volunteering to come here.

ME: Great. Leave it to me to pick the worst planet to live on. I have about a billion other questions, but I promise to save those for book two. Can I at least ask about crop circles?

HS: Some are fraudulent. The authentic ones are actually beams of healing energy from other worlds, trying to help you by sending their love to your planet. If you could understand the symbols, you would be profoundly moved by their poetic beauty and deep love for you.

ME: That's so awesome. So just to be sure, there are no more abductions taking place?

HS: Correct. Absolutely none. The next contact will be widely public, peaceful, and loving. There are no monsters out there waiting to take over earth and annihilate the human race. Although, you may still see strange things in the sky from time to time- you are being closely and carefully watched by an entire Superuniverse of over one trillion life-bearing planets, many of which are currently inhabited by highly advanced civilizations. They wait with baited breath as you make your collective spiritual leap. Your unassuming little blue planet has the attention of an unimaginable host of beings. Though you cannot yet see them, many are near your planet now; hovering in the level of vibration just above yours.

ME: That's rather mind blowing. Can I ask just one more question? What do they look like? Are there any giant squids, bugs, blobs, or whatever?

HS: No. All intelligent creatures with the capacity to worship our Creator, have an upright bipedal, humanoid form. However, they can vary in shape, color, style and size. Some look quite different from you, while others look almost the same, but remember: they are in this illusion too, and you must learn to forgive their form and see only the Light of the Holy Spirit within them- just as you must do with your fellow human beings here on earth.

ME: That sounds like quite an obstacle. I mean, we currently have a lot of trouble accepting our *own* differing skin colors, cultures, and weight and body types. We judge *everything* about one another's bodies. We have a long way to go.

HS: My Way is short. You have only to take My Hand, and I will lead you.

ME: That sounds poetic and beautiful, but I'm still having trouble doing that in a realistic sense. I wish aliens would just make contact with us now. We could really use their help.

HS: They know that if they made open contact now, your people would either unduly revere them, or despise them. In either case, the reaction would be inappropriate. They are creations of God equal to you, and the only appropriate reaction to them is one of *unconditional love for the Spirit within them*. Your planet is not ready for that yet, and so you must wait. Too many of you still do not truly believe that God goes with each of you, wherever you go. He is living within each and every one of you and you continue to search outside yourselves where you will never find Him. Learn to love Him within each other, and you will have found what you so desperately seek. Then the universe of Love and Light will open up to your planet.

Chapter 9: Lessons 41-45

The Four Horsemen and The Four Obstacles To Peace

41. God goes with me wherever I go.

HS: The more certain you become of the truth of your unity in God, the more you will actually feel Him as you go about your daily business. He will become your strength, and His Vision a gift to you.

42. God is my strength. Vision is His gift.

HS: With the awareness of His Presence, comes not only His Love, but His strength, and all His other gifts. The gift of His Vision is always with you. He is your Source. You cannot see apart from Him.

43. God is my Source. I cannot see apart from Him.

HS: The gift of His Vision is the ability to see Him in all living things. It is to know that underneath the material world, there lies the Life Force of God. He is your Source and you cannot see apart from Him. He is the light in which you see.

44. God is the light in which I see.

HS: So far, all you've been able to see is illusion. You've seen nothing real in this darkness, but I will help you correct that, through using the light of My Inner Vision. Use My mind to think and I will turn on the light so that you may see at last.

45. God is the Mind with which I think.

HS: You have no other mind, but the one you share with Me. When you recognize this fact, I will direct you according to My Will, and My Will is that you accept My love, peace and unity.

. . .

ME: Okay, I get that I can see only bodies with my bodily eyes, because my body is part of the illusion. What I still don't understand is how to see with my "inner spiritual eyes." I mean, I try to look at people and say to myself, "Spirit is contained within that body. It's not who they are." I say this to myself, but I don't *feel* it. Nothing about them seems to change or become different for me. If they're irritating me, they remain irritating.

HS: Let's review the four obstacles to peace once again, this time in order.

ME: Alright. Here they are all together:

    A. The First Obstacle to Peace: The Desire to Get Rid of It.
    B. The Second Obstacle to Peace: The Belief the Body is Valuable for What It Offers.
    C. The Third Obstacle to Peace: The Attraction of Death.
    D. The Fourth Obstacle to Peace: The Fear of God.

HS: The first obstacle is your desire to get rid of peace by crucifying your fellow brothers. You do this every time you attack someone outwardly or in your mind. When you think unloving thoughts towards others, you are attacking Me. I am in them, and as long as you see them as bodies capable of causing you pain and suffering, you will have unloving thoughts about them. In this way, you demonstrate that you do not want peace and try to get rid of it through some form of attack or defense. Do not have attack thoughts about *yourself* either, because I am in you as well. Do not try to crucify Me through hating bodies; you cannot kill God.

Your second obstacle is the belief the body is valuable for what it offers. What has the body brought you besides suffering? You may think it contains joy, but it is fleeting. All bodies die. There is no getting around that. Do not value the perishable. Do not let it come between Me and you. We are eternal.

Your third obstacle to peace is the attraction of death. Your fear of death stands between you and peace, but fear it not. It is only a *dream* of death. Your lives are lived with the fear of death running in the background. You could die at any moment; from anything. You are obsessed with death. On one hand you abuse yourself, enticing an early "end" and on the other hand you cling to the body as though its life is yours. Let this all go. You are each a part of God's holy Sonship and can never die. Death of the body is a comfortable, sweet transition into Life. That is all.

Your fourth and final obstacle to peace is the fear of God Himself. You fear His wrath and punishment because you feel guilty for having come into this illusion. Deep down, you think you've done something wrong. Here then, is the last thing you must learn to remember: you *do* love God, and you *do* want Him, and have done nothing to offend Him. The fear of this remembrance lies in the fact that, if you allowed yourself this memory, all you see before your eyes would disappear. You'd literally transcend this world and return to Me. You fear this. You fear to see your brothers and yourself as One, because it would mean giving up all you never had. Dear child, you give up nothing in exchange for everything. See no sin (separation) between yourself and your fellows. You need not fear your Oneness.

ME: So, I have four fears posing as obstacles to my peace. They are:

1.) Peace
2.) The body
3.) Death
4.) God

For some reason this reminds me of the four horsemen of the apocalypse from the bible.

HS: They are the same.

ME: You're kidding. Do You want me to go find this quote?

HS: No. You may read it, but it is filled with fear, written from the standpoint of the ego. This section of the bible describes the ego's demise, not your own, and presenting it here would only increase fear rather than allay it. Increasing fear is never My objective. Just know that each of the horsemen represents each one of the four fears listed above. You will overcome each of them through love and forgiveness.

ME: I looked it up. It's found in Revelations 6, Holy Bible, King James Version. And yeah, it's a terrifying read.

The Four Horsemen are:

1. War (we overcome with the peace of forgiveness).
2. Power (we overcome the idea we are a body).
3. Justice/Revenge (we overcome through understanding there has been no wrongdoing).
4. Death (we overcome by accepting we are eternal Life).

Overall, this bible passage reads like the world ends in apocalyptic fiery damnation and hell.

HS: Again, I restate that this passage was written from the standpoint of the ego. It quakes at the thought of its own demise. Just know that as these four fears are overcome through love and forgiveness; as the barriers between you and I become less and less; life will improve for you drastically. This will manifest as positive changes in your personal life, your world, and even your entire universe. The world will not end in a fiery apocalypse; it will find a new loving beginning.

ME: Now we're talking. That's all I want! Positive changes in my life and in the world. How do I bring these barriers down again? Seriously, I know You've told me, but please tell me again? Just to be clear.

HS: Through knowing God is the Love in which you forgive.

Chapter 10: Lessons 46-50

Forgiveness Is Our Business

46. God is the Love in which I forgive.

HS: You are not asked to perform the seemingly difficult task of forgiving illusions alone. We will overcome them together. Trust in My strength.

47. God is the strength in which I trust.

HS: The process of forgiveness appears difficult because your body's senses are so overpowering that you think it is impossible to see past what the world is showing you. Trust in My strength to see you through the difficult moments, when the illusion seems real to you. You have nothing to fear.

48. There is nothing to fear.

HS: Remember that you are forever safe, and I will never leave you. My strength is your own and you have nothing to fear. Do not listen to the ego, who insists you are a body; frail, sick, weak and dying. Listen instead to the quiet loving whisper of My Voice, Who says none of this is so; you are complete and healed and whole. You are My Perfect Son. Listen to Me speak to you like this all through the day.

49. God's Voice speaks to me all through the day.

HS: My Voice never leaves you; I am always speaking to you. It is only you who choose not to hear Me. Be still and listen. Hear My Voice speak to you only of My divine love for you, your total safety in My Arms, and your perfect innocence. I sustain you with My Love.

50. I am sustained by the Love of God.

HS: It is I Who sustains you beyond the death of your temporary body. You are the Light of the world; created in My Love, and cannot be harmed, cannot die, and will forever remain My Holy Son.

. . .

ME: So it all comes down to forgiving this illusion and going Home. That's our only job here? Our only purpose?

HS: Correct. However, it may help you to understand exactly what it means to forgive.

ME: I'm all ears.

HS: I have explained to you that "sin" is not an act that I would ever punish, but rather, it is simply an error in thought; the error of the idea of separation from Me. Sin by this definition requires correction through *forgiveness*, not punishment. This is a form of forgiveness few understand.

ME: I feel a quote coming on. Let me guess. You want me to go find the definition of forgiveness as found in the ACIM?

HS: Now would be a good time to do that, yes.

The following quotation from the Course is from WORKBOOK Part II — 1. What Is Forgiveness?

"Forgiveness recognizes what you thought your brother did to you has not occurred. It does not pardon sins and make them real. It sees there was no sin. And in that view are all your sins forgiven. What is sin, except a false idea about God's Son? Forgiveness merely sees its falsity, and therefore lets it go. What then is free to take its place is now the Will of God." (1:1-7)

HS: To truly forgive, means that you see one another as *though nothing has ever happened to you*. There is no past between you. The world forgives by seeing the error someone committed against you, pardons it (thus making it real), then says "I will overlook this, but secretly let us never forget it happened." God forgives you as though nothing happened to you to begin with. Because nothing ever has. Your slate is not only clean, but He says it was never dirty to begin with.

ME: I don't think anyone on the planet can forgive like that. It seems impossible to forgive the entire past in people. I'm just thinking of all the people who've been abused, not to mention all the small stuff that irritates me on a daily basis.

HS: Yet, I am asking that you forgive so deeply that not one person is excluded from your love. Not one thought of hatred or attack is held towards anyone. This is how I love you. You have no past. There is, and ever shall be, only the present moment, where you are perfect, innocent, and whole; as God created you.

ME: Love and forgiveness on that level sounds impossible! Insane!

HS: Find Me the quote where I explain that this is *not* insane. In fact, it is through forgiveness that you find your sanity at long last. You must welcome Me in every person, *or you do not welcome Me at all.*

The following quotation from the Course is from TEXT Chapter 13 — III. The Fear of Redemption

"But exempt no one from your love, or you will be hiding a dark place in your mind where the Holy Spirit is not welcome. And thus you will exempt yourself from His healing power, for by not offering total love you will not be healed completely." (9:2-3)

HS: There can be no exceptions to your love for one another. It is either whole, or it is not. It cannot be partial or you will not find healing and happiness.

ME: How do we achieve love like Yours? I can't believe anyone in the world knows how to love like You.

HS: Through practicing the holy instant. Please insert the simple instructions for practicing that now.

The following quotation from the Course is from TEXT Chapter 15 — IV. Practicing the Holy Instant

"The necessary condition for the holy instant does not require that you have no thoughts that are not pure. But it does require that you have none that you would keep." (9:1-2)

HS: Do you see how easy this practice is? Simply forgive all unloving thoughts as soon as they arise. Let them go. Do not believe they are true. That is all I am asking. This will be enough for you to step aside and let Me lead the way.

ME: I guess I can do that. Although I'm afraid my mind will be so preoccupied with forgiving unloving thoughts, there won't be room to think about anything else.

HS: That's the idea. I will then replace your old ego thoughts, with My Thoughts of Love and Light. You will undergo a divine revelation of truth. You will remember you are the light of world.

Chapter 11: Lessons 61-80

Deciding For Happiness

61. I am the light of the world.

62. Forgiveness is my function as the light of the world.

HS: You are the light of God as He extends Himself. When you feel hate, fear, or hold grievances, you obscure this beautiful light as though you've hidden it under a basket. Your vibration darkens down to that of the ego. This happens to all of you, most of the time. To pull up into the vibration of God's Light, you need only be aware of your One Self. This is the aspect of your Self that *observes what the ego is doing*. This is You as the Watcher. Simply step back into this space and observe how the ego is ruining your happiness. The peace and quiet experienced within this space is what forgiveness feels like. *Forgiveness is your function as the light of the world. You are the light of the world*. Once you've disconnected yourself from the ego by moving into the "observer" perspective, you have removed the basket from God's Light. Your light brings peace to every mind through your forgiveness. Do not forget this is your function.

63. The light of the world brings peace to every mind through my forgiveness.

64. Let me not forget my function.

HS: Once you have lifted the barrier to your light, you can extend this light as peace to others through forgiveness. *The light of the world brings peace to every mind through your forgiveness*. This light is either shared or obscured through your thoughts, so it is important that you become vigilant over your mind. At first, you may have to constantly remind yourself to step back into your Self as the Observer. But over time, with practice, this will begin to happen naturally. *Forget not your function*. It is just as easy to make the small shift back up, as it is to slip down. There is no harm in going back and forth, but as you practice, you will desire to spend more and more time in the higher vibration with God. You will only want to perform the function He gave you.

This is what brings you true happiness.

65. My only function is the one God gave me.

66. My happiness and my function are one.

HS: There is nothing else you are expected to do while down here on earth. Everyone seems to ask, "Why am I here? What is the meaning of my life? What should I be doing?"

This is it.

Just this one thing all day long, as you go about your worldly business. Practice shifting up into your higher Self to the perspective of observer through forgiveness. Neither the world nor your ego can give you purpose. *Your only function is the one God gave you.* As you perform this function of forgiveness, you realize, you're much happier! It feels good to experience life through the eyes of Christ rather than the ego. This is not the same as withdrawal. To withdraw, means you no longer participate at all; you've "checked out." You're actually "checking in" for the first time in your life when you shift your perspective inward. You will know when you've shifted, because you will feel a sense of happiness. This feeling of happiness is forgiveness, and forgiveness is your only function. *Your happiness and your function are one.* It is happiness to perform your function of loving, because you *are* love. Love created you like itself, and love holds no grievances.

67. Love created me like itself.

68. Love holds no grievances.

HS: *God is Love and He created you like Himself.* You are love, and you are wholly loving and kind. Only the ego sees condemnation. *Love holds no grievances.* Only the ego thinks it can be damaged in any way. When you hold grievances, the light of the world is hidden from your eyes. It is up to you to choose to see it. In this way, your salvation comes from yourself.

69. My grievances hide the light of the world in me.

70. My salvation comes from me.

HS: All negative thoughts come from the ego. These thoughts take your attention away from your True Self. *Your grievances hide the light of the world in you.* When you let go of all grievances, you step aside and allow your Self to shine. This feels like sweet salvation. *Your salvation comes from you.* Only you can make this choice. God will not force Himself upon you; you have to openly welcome Him through letting your grievances go. This is His plan, and only His plan for your salvation will work.

71. Only God's plan for salvation will work.

72. Holding grievances is an attack on God's plan for salvation.

HS: God's plan for salvation is peace, and *only God's plan for salvation will work.* If what you see upsets you, you are not at peace. This is an obvious truth. Therefore, *holding grievances is an attack on God's plan for salvation.* Do not keep even the smallest irritation in your mind. These tiny dark thoughts keep the light of heaven from you. Remember- you are not in *denial* over having these dark thoughts. Simply *note* that you're having them, and be willing to let them go. There is a difference. It is your will there be light, and this is God's Will also.

73. I will there be light.

74. There is no will but God's.

HS: When you struggle with your small irritations and repetitive negative thoughts, remember Who You Really Are. Remember how much power you have. You have the power to make a world of darkness, and you also have the power to undo it. *Will there be light.* You share this will with God, and *there is no will but God's;* and what He Wills, shall be done. You can delay, but not prevent, the light from coming. You are under no other laws but God's.

75. The light has come.

76. I am under no laws but God's.

HS: Only what is eternal is real, and God creates only what is eternal. The light He created has never gone away, because it is eternal. *The light has come.* You can change what you experience here within the illusion by deciding to acknowledge the eternal in all you see. You do not have to obey the laws of this world; they are based upon a false reality. *You are under no laws but God's.* His, is the law of Love, which creates only miracles. Being His, you are entitled to His miracles. Let miracles replace all grievances.

77. I am entitled to miracles.

78. Let miracles replace all grievances.

HS: You want what lies beyond this world. You want the love, peace, and happiness that salvation from this level of existence brings. The only way to achieve it, is to accept what God is offering you, and He offers you only miracles. *You are entitled to miracles.* To accept His peace in exchange for attack, is a miracle. *Let miracles replace all grievances.* You are unaware of your Oneness. You do not recognize that this lack of awareness is the only problem you've ever had, and you cannot solve a problem you do not recognize.

79. Let me recognize the problem so it can be solved.

80. Let me recognize my problems have been solved.

HS: Do not be deceived. It appears that you have thousands of problems! Even as one seems to be solved, another host of them replaces it. It seems there is no end to the parade of problems that assail you. All forms of discomfort are the result of your seeming separation from God. You must *recognize the problem so it can be solved.* Where did this problem originate from? The only logical place- your mind. The second you imagined yourself split apart from God, He provided the immediate solution. He gave you the ability to remember the Atonement: your Oneness. *Recognize your problems have been solved.* The correction has already been made, because you never left Him to begin with.

. . .

ME: It seems like a lot of work to watch my thoughts all the time. I mean, I don't *really* want to choose against You. Why can't You just see that, and fix everything? Why can't You just look at all our suffering and zap us Home again? You know we don't want pain. We want to be experiencing Heaven. Make that happen for us!

HS: I *do* know this. However, I cannot emphasize enough, that I will not give you what you do not ask for. You do not want My peace because you are not choosing it. You are continually deciding against your own happiness through choosing conflict. There is a quote from the ACIM about this, and I'd like you to insert it here now.

ME: I know exactly which one You're talking about, and I have a question about that. I have a document with over 100 pages of quotes I've collected from the Course. There's no way I've memorized them all. Yet, once we start these discussions, the appropriate ones mysteriously seem to pop into my head. Is that You're doing? It was the same thing with those bible references. They just suddenly came into my mind, when I haven't opened the bible in 25 years. I had very little idea as to what they were about, yet there they were.

HS: Yes, I am able to inspire you to remember what you seem to have forgotten. I am not *controlling* your mind; only *inspiring* it. It is up to you whether or not you want to listen.

ME: Well I think that's just kind of... Weird. In fact, this whole conversation is weird. I'm probably crazy.

HS: You think this conversation is strange, and that you may be insane, yet I assure you; this is the first sane thing you've ever done in your life.

ME: Well now *that's* probably true.

HS: It is both normal, sane, and completely natural for you to communicate with Me. It is this very communication that these lessons are aimed at reestablishing. Your acceptances of the teachings from the Course are why you are able to hear Me to begin with. It is this communication that you want to help others learn to reestablish. Please insert the quote that addresses the question of why most people can't seem to decide for their happiness, and hear Me once again.

The following quotations from the Course are from TEXT Chapter 21 — VII. The Last Unanswered Question

"No one decides against his happiness, but he may do so if he does not see he does it. And if he sees his happiness as ever changing, now this, now that, and now an elusive shadow attached to nothing, he does decide against it." (12:5-6)

"Joy cannot be perceived except through constant vision. And constant vision can be given only those who wish for constancy. The power of the Son of God's desire remains the proof that he is wrong who sees himself as helpless. Desire what you want, and you will look on it and think it real. No thought but this has the power to release or kill. And none can leave the thinker's mind, or leave him unaffected." (13:3-8)

HS: You do not even realize you are choosing hell over Heaven. You are not aware of what your thoughts are doing, and until you are, you will continue to make the same mistaken choice over and over again. You are not at the mercy of the world you see. The world you see, is at the mercy of you. You have decided that this world can bring you happiness, and you've died trying to find it each and every time. Yet, the world will always fail you. To stop this mad chase, you must decide you are not helpless. You have the power to change what you see, by changing who you think you are. Are you a body or My holy Son? One identity will seem to kill you, and one will release you. Neither thought about yourself will leave you unaffected. You must decide who you are, and only one choice brings you miracles. And miracles can only be seen in light.

Chapter 12: Lessons 91-110

Forgiving Abuse

91. Miracles are seen in light.
92. Miracles are seen in light, and light and strength are one.

HS: How do you "turn on the light" in order to see miracles? The light "turns on" when you finally decide to forgive the separation between yourself and Me. A miracle happens every time you consciously decide to step back from your reactive ego self and forgive instead of condemn; when you recognize that this is a dream and you are safe at Home in God. A miracle is to remember that you have the power to choose whether to feel pain or love. It is a miracle every time you love your brother as yourself. These are all miracles. This is how My light is turned on before your very eyes. Miracles bring not a physical worldly light, but an inner light. *Miracles are seen in light.* Seeing miracles in My light may sound impossible, but I have given you My Strength to do it. *Miracles are seen in light, and light and strength are one.* My light and joy and peace abide in you, because this is how I created you.

93. Light and joy and peace abide in me.
94. I am as God created me.

HS: You do not see that *light and joy and peace abide in you.* You haven't changed into something else simply because you see yourself as a body. *You are as God created you,* and so you shall forever remain. Nothing has changed except your decision to see something other than the truth about your one Self, united with your Creator; and salvation comes from your one Self.

95. I am one Self, united with my Creator.
96. Salvation comes from my one Self.

HS: Every time you choose to feel attack, fear, hate, or judgement, you are choosing to resist the Truth. You are seeing another as a body, and perpetuating the illusion. To undo this choice, you must forgive it. Remember instead that *you are one Self, united with your Creator.* In this thought, your salvation lies. *Salvation comes from your one Self.* It's up to you to decide you are spirit. Accept this part in My plan for your salvation.

97. I am spirit.

98. I will accept my part in God's plan for salvation.

HS: Know *you are spirit.* Accept this now, and fulfill your part in My plan for salvation. It is no small part. It is no small thing to deny the seeming reality of this world in exchange for another. Yet, who can long deny My Will? God's Will be done. *You will accept your part in God's plan for salvation.* You had to deny your Self in order to experience what you are not, and hell became your reality. Now you must deny hell, in order to remember Heaven. This is your only job. Salvation is your only function here. Your part is essential to My plan for salvation.

99. Salvation is my only function here.

100. My part is essential to God's plan for salvation.

HS: *Salvation is your only function here.* Each and every person must make the journey to salvation. No one can escape it or do it for you. Others can show you the way, but *your part is essential to God's plan for salvation.* I do not want you to suffer. My Will for you is perfect happiness, and you share My Will.

101. God's Will for me is perfect happiness.

102. I share God's Will for happiness for me.

HS: I know you are dreaming a nightmare. God hears your cry for help through Me, for I am the liaison between you and Him. And He answered you instantly with His call for you to return to His love and happiness. *God's Will for you is perfect happiness. You share God's Will for happiness for you.* God is both Love and happiness. It is this you seek. You are only seeking for what belongs to you in truth.

103. God, being Love, is also happiness.

104. I seek but what belongs to me in truth.

HS: When you bring your will into alignment with God, you begin to create *with* Him. Like hearing a song, and joining your voice to it, you add your light, joy, and peace to the chorus of Heaven. As you heal your mind of the idea of separation, the space those ideas left behind is filled with the love and happiness of God. This is what finding God feels like. *God, being Love, is also happiness.* It is this deep happiness you seek, and it belongs to you. *You seek what belongs to you in truth.* His peace and joy are yours, so be still and listen to this truth within.

105. God's peace and joy are mine.

106. Let me be still and listen to the truth.

HS: You are entitled to happiness, and it comes along with Unity in Him. *God's peace and joy are yours.* How do you accept them? You can only hear His Voice and accept your happiness, when you still the voice of the ego. *Be still and listen to the truth.* For the truth of your Oneness will correct all errors in your mind. Give the gift of truth and you will receive it.

107. Truth will correct all errors in my mind.

108. To give and to receive are one in truth.

HS: The truth of your Oneness will correct the error of separation in your mind. You invite the truth when you decide to see Christ in one another. *This truth will correct all errors in your mind.* Let your mind rest in this gift you give, for as you give it, you will receive it. *To give and to receive are one in truth.* The truth is, you all rest in God, for that is how He created you to be.

109. I rest in God.

110. I am as God created me.

Start Here

HS: When a child dreams a nightmare, the parent does not punish or become angry with the child for what they did in their dream, no matter how horrible. The parent lovingly tells the child they have done no wrong, and have been resting in peace and safety the entire time they dreamt. So are you now. You dream terrible things, but in reality, *you rest in God*. Nothing about you has changed. You are not condemned for anything. No one has ever harmed you, no one has been wronged. *You remain as God created you,* despite what you may dream.

· · ·

ME: I'm struggling to accept this whole idea that everything that's happened to us is just a dream. I'm thinking about all those out in the world who've suffered abuse of any kind. How can we just let that go? Where's the accountability for those who've caused pain in others? Where's the justice? I think this idea of "forgiving the past as though it never happened" is *insulting* to victims. It's downplaying their very real suffering at the hands of others. It seems degrading and disrespectful to them somehow.

HS: Forgiveness does not downplay or degrade *any* of the hardships you have all seemingly suffered. Let Me explain it to you like this: you've heard the phrase that "all the world is a stage, and you are but actors." This is true in a very real sense. This world is not real; it is all an act. You have each previously agreed on what roles you're willing to play for one another before coming here. And just like a play, no one is actually hurt, but the situations *do* appear extremely real. Yet, when an actor "dies" on stage, they are not really dead; they simply walk offstage and return to the real world. So is it true with death and suffering in your world. No one dies, no one is hurt. It *seems* that way, and your experiences *appear* real, but I assure you; your experiences only have value as far as your spiritual growth is concerned. You are learning real lessons, but without any real damage. You are not your bodies, you are Spirit. You will not fully realize this until you've "walked offstage" to God's real world, through forgiveness of this one.

ME: Okay. I get all that. But why does the script have to be so *bad?*

HS: You can put down the script any time you want. Just simply see the truth. No one has ever really hurt you. They are simply playing the part *you've asked them to play,* in order for you to learn what *you've asked them to teach you.* Let Me further clarify.

All of the people in your life, from the very beginning of your birth and on until your body's death, are playing a role for you. Nothing happens at random, but you have the free will to respond to these scenarios in any way you choose. So, for instance, if you were born into a family with an abusive parent, you chose this situation on purpose, given what it was you said you wanted to learn. You chose this from a higher place, and then forgot you made this choice. That may seem hard to believe. I understand. No one wants to believe that babies have *chosen* to have cancer or that anyone has *chosen* any form of suffering. Be that as it may, it is entirely up to you how you play this drama out. Everyone is playing the part you asked them to, and you are playing yours. Everyone is playing their part so perfectly in fact, that you are each convinced that this is who you are. It's completely unapparent to you, that underneath the volatile people you encounter, are beautiful beings of love and light, who volunteered to suffer through their role for you. You are also playing your part to the letter for them. Now it is up to *you* whether that part is one that perpetuates the ego and fear, or demonstrates that you are the champion of love and forgiveness; a holy Son of God. The key to achieving forgiveness lies in the ability to see others as the actor that they are. Thank them gratefully for taking on such a difficult role and then let their character go. Put down the script. You don't have to react to anything they may say or do, because it's simply not true.

ME: So everyone is doing exactly as we've asked, from our parents and siblings, all the way down to the rude grocery store clerk we'll never see again? We should thank them for playing their role in our spiritual awakening?

HS: Yes. Everyone you interact with will cause you to make a choice. You must make a choice between reacting from your ego with negativity or seeing them through the eyes of the Holy Spirit with love. The whole point of this "stage" is to consistently choose love over anything else. All the people in your lives are driving you ever and anon towards God. You are doing the same for them. You're all here to help each other move into a higher reality. That's what the "contrast" between peace and pain is for; to begin to see the difference and know for sure what you want. You want God. God is peace and love. This is what you, and every person in your life wants.

ME: So all the people in my life are here just to drive me nuts in order to provide me with the practice I need in order to learn I want peace instead of pain?

HS: Yes, but you learn it in the safety of this world of illusion where nothing is real but the love of God within you. This Love you share with God will never pass away, cannot be damaged, and is impossible to sever. It is the *realization* of this Love that you seek. Because your ego blocks it from your view, you feel loneliness. You feel separate from one another. You each then try to fill that void with "special" relationships or other endless external means in the hopes of filling the lack. While you still see through the eyes of the ego, you will continue to try to separate out those that you hate, from those whom you love. While you desire to see differences, you will not see Christ, and will not know your Union.

ME: I suppose I can try to see Christ in those around me. I mean, I don't want to feel awful later in Heaven for the way I treated "beautiful beings of love and light" while they were under the guise of abusive jerks in my life.

HS: In situations you find it difficult or downright impossible to forgive, remember that you are asked only to step back from the "realness" of the situation; remember that you do not understand anything you see. You do not know the deep past, nor the outcome in the far future of any of your relationships. You are seeing things from the narrow perspective of time here within the illusion. You do not know what past lives you've lived together, or how many roles have been previously reversed. Your roles may reverse yet again, or this may be the life of your forgiveness and reconciliation; thus ending the cycle. You do not know. You cannot see anyone as they truly are. Do not judge whom you do not understand. You are blind to the Holy Spirit within them. They are your savior as you learn to forgive yourself for failing to see past their bodily form. You will eventually experience for yourself what you have done to others. What you do to them, will always be returned to you; if not in this life, then in the next. There is no greater reason to be kind to others, than this.

ME: So that's all forgiveness asks us to do? Simply admit we don't understand anything we see; that we might have been wrong in our judgment, and that there is more to the story than we know?

HS: Correct. As you are now, you cannot see anything as it exists in eternity. Forgiveness of what you see wrongly here, teaches you how to unlock eternity in all things. This is the key to happiness. Forgiveness offers everything you want.

Chapter 13: Lessons 121-140

Guns, Eating Meat, Deforestation, and Abortion

121. Forgiveness is the key to happiness.
122. Forgiveness offers everything I want.

HS: You are not here to suffer through endless, meaningless tasks associated with the body. Yet, you can't avoid all the endless, meaningless tasks associated with it either. You are only asked to let go of the *idea* of your being a body. The thoughts that preoccupy your mind about the body are not real, because your body is not real. *Your mind holds only what you think with God.* The thoughts you think with God are the only true thoughts you have. Welcome these thoughts through forgiving the illusion of your body, and you will know My Thoughts of happiness. This is all you want. *Forgiveness is the key to happiness, and forgiveness offers everything you want.* These are the gifts of your Father; be grateful for them. Remember your Oneness with God and thank Him for it.

123. I thank my Father for His gifts to me.
124. Let me remember I am one with God.

HS: God has given you the power to create as He does. *Thank Your Father for His gifts to you.* You have inherited His gifts because you are One with Him. Never forget this. *Remember you are one with God.* It is only when you quiet your thoughts about this world, that you are able to receive His Word and know that all you give is given to your One Self.

125. In quiet I receive God's Word today.
126. All that I give is given to myself.

HS: Peace is the state of God's mind. It is through conforming to this state, that you are able to consciously hear Him. To do this, you must silence all thoughts you hold about the world. *In quiet you receive God's Word.* When you receive His Word, you simultaneously become a giver of His Love to everyone else in your One Self. *All that you give is given to yourself.* It cannot be any other way. You share One Mind, One Self, and One Love. There is no other Love, than the One Love of God.

127. There is no love but God's.

128. The world I see holds nothing that I want.

HS: There is nothing to give to your One Mind but God's Love. *There is no love but God's.* There is nothing else. There is nothing to be found in the world outside of you. *The world you see holds nothing that you want.* God is patiently waiting for you to look in every relationship or worldly acquisition, to discover this for yourself and come Home to Him at last. He waits for you to realize that you want a world beyond this one. Until then, it is impossible to see two worlds.

129. Beyond this world there is a world I want.

130. It is impossible to see two worlds.

HS: *Beyond this world there is a world you want.* You must see the world around you with forgiveness, thus denying its reality, because *it is impossible to see two worlds.* You cannot be in two places at once. You are either in Heaven or hell. You cannot serve two masters. Your choice is determined by your thoughts. Thoughts of attack and anger will keep you in this illusion, while thoughts of love and forgiveness will ascend your mind to God's Thoughts, and you will see Heaven. This is the truth you seek, and you cannot fail to find it. Loose the world from all you think it is.

131. No one can fail who seeks to reach the truth.

132. I loose the world from all I thought it was.

HS: You seek to regain your remembrance of God. You seek to regain Heaven and your peace, and you cannot fail. *No one can fail who seeks to reach the truth.* But first you must *loose the world from all you thought it was.* It is an illusion. Bodies die, mountains crumble, and even planets eventually meet their end. They have no eternal value. But Spirit is eternal, and this is what you are. Do not value what is valueless. Perceive the valueless with forgiveness.

133. I will not value what is valueless.

134. Let me perceive forgiveness as it is.

HS: Enjoy this world for the time you experience it, but *do not value what is valueless*. The only possible way to live here, while simultaneously becoming aware of Heaven, is through forgiveness. Forgiveness allows all things to pass before your eyes without reaction or possession. *Perceive forgiveness as it is*. Forgiveness is the undoing of your value in the unreal. When what you perceive is unreal to you, you do not get upset over anything you see happening. If you feel the need to defend yourself, it means you see yourself as a body capable of suffering attack. Even sickness is a defense against the truth of Who You Are.

135. If I defend myself I am attacked.

136. Sickness is a defense against the truth.

HS: Defense of any kind, is an indication you have fallen into the illusion of being a body. *If you defend yourself you are attacked*. When you defend, you've made the illusion real to you. Your body then responds to these attack thoughts through manifesting sickness. Cells, bacteria, and viruses all do battle against one another in conflict on a microscopic scale, reflecting your thoughts. *Sickness is a defense against the truth*. Heal your thoughts, and you heal your body. You are not sick. You are healed and whole, safe from all forms of attack and completely at peace. Remember this and the attack is called off, and you are healed. And you are never healed alone. Heaven is the decision you must make.

137. When I am healed I am not healed alone.

138. Heaven is the decision I must make.

HS: You need only heal one thought, and all else will be healed along with it. *When you are healed, you are not healed alone*. Heal your thought of separation; know you are One. To heal through this thought, is to resolve every conflict once and for all. Once done, Heaven will be made manifest on earth. Until then, in every conflict you encounter, *Heaven is the decision you must make.* Through making this decision, you accept the Atonement for yourself. Atonement is salvation, and only salvation can be said to cure.

139. I will accept Atonement for myself.

140. Only salvation can be said to cure.

HS: Herein lies your power. You have the power to choose to *accept Atonement for yourself.* Atonement is the state of Total Oneness. Through unforgiveness you left God, and experienced a world of separation. Now, through forgiveness, you have the power to undo this choice and choose salvation. This is the only cure for all that is wrong with you and the world. *Only salvation can be said to cure.*

. . .

ME: You said we have to forgive all things we see here, because it is illusion and forgiveness is the way to correct it. Alright, I get that. However, I have some areas of concern. There are certain topics that cause a lot of conflict between people. It would be great if You could just tell me the right way to think about them. For instance, how do You feel about gun control and abortion? Is it okay to eat meat and cut down forests? I mean, we still have to live here, so how do You want me to see these things?

HS: You said it yourself; this is all an illusion, and therefore, nothing matters. Therefore, all choices are correct.

ME: That can't be possible. I don't accept that answer. If You can see me, please note my disappointed face.

HS: I *can* see you, and *don't* be disappointed. I am Love, and can only look on all things lovingly. There is no other way to see the world. All choices either bring you closer to Me, or drive you further away, but you can never *get* away. I'm not worried about any of you failing in your choice for Me. So, I am "for" any choice that you make. The problem is, you do not always recognize what choices bring you closer to Me and which ones take you further away. Please find the appropriate quote regarding this, and insert it here.

ME: Yep, just thought of it. And that's still weird. So after this, would You please give me a clearer answer to my previous questions?

HS: I will do that.

The following quotation from the Course is from TEXT Chapter 18 — V. The Happy Dream

"If you already understood the difference between truth and illusion, the Atonement would have no meaning. The holy instant, the holy relationship, and the Holy Spirit's teaching, and all the means by which salvation is accomplished, would have no purpose. For they are all but aspects of the plan to change your dreams of fear to happy dreams, from which you waken easily to knowledge. Put yourself not in charge of this, for you cannot distinguish between advance and retreat. Some of your greatest advances you have judged as failures, and some of your deepest retreats you have evaluated as success." (1:2-6)

ME: Alright, so which choices are advances and which ones are failures?

HS: Again, your choices are neither "good" nor "bad;" they do not matter in terms of anger or punishment from Me. A good rule to follow is this: nothing within this dream should be used to increase guilt or fear in anyone else; be it guns, abortions, eating meat or cutting down trees. All living things should be loved and respected, for I am within them all. *However, that does not mean you should not use them.* Guns are perfectly fine to own and use, unless they are used to terrorize. You'd be surprised to know that animals actually don't mind being your food, but they would prefer not to live lives of suffering beforehand. Trees also don't mind being used by you for your needs, but do not waste them. See what I am saying? Be respectful, kind and loving in all you do, and you will find your way to Me.

ME: Yeah, but a lot of people aren't respectful, kind and loving in all they do. What should we do about *them*?

HS: Don't worry about them. Worry only about yourself, and whether or not you're seeing them lovingly; no matter what choices they seem to be making. Do this, and you will bring more light to the world and yourself than you could ever know. You will literally light up your mind.

ME: I suppose I could manage that. With a lot of practice.

HS: I am now going to share something shocking with you. Are you ready?

ME: Gimme a second. You've surprised me before, and as impossible as this sounds to my own ears, I never seem to know what You're going to say next. So I'm taking Your warning seriously. Okay. I'm ready.

HS: Three "lifetimes" ago, *you* were once an aborted fetus.

ME: Yep. You were right. That's a shocking thing to say to me. And You're telling me this *why*?

HS: How do you feel about this right now, this instant? Are you currently damaged by that experience in any way?

ME: Well, if I truly take stock of myself, I guess I'm fine. I mean, I don't remember that happening to me of course, so I don't feel anything about it. And obviously I'm alive right now, so it didn't actually kill me. How did I feel about it when it happened?

HS: You were as fine with it then, as you are now. In fact, you *volunteered* for it- happily and without hesitation.

ME: Why would I do that?

HS: You dearly love the soul who needed that experience. It was your gift to them. It was no sacrifice for you to enter into the dream for a little while, just to help with this forgiveness lesson.

ME: I can't hardly believe that something like that happened to me. I feel absolutely no damage from it; it's as though it never happened.

HS: This is because you cannot *be* damaged, lost, broken or killed. You are always and forever in the unchanging state of Life. This is also why, ultimately,

91

there is no such thing as reincarnation, because there is never any disruption in your One Life. You are all continuously alive. You can never really die or go anywhere. No one is damaged by the death of the body. You are each simply having serial experiences within the illusion of birth and death.

The following quotations from the Course are from
MANUAL FOR TEACHERS
24. Is Reincarnation So?

"In the ultimate sense, reincarnation is impossible. There is no past or future, and the idea of birth into a body has no meaning either once or many times." (1:1-2)

"Does this mean that the teacher of God should not believe in reincarnation himself, or discuss it with others who do? The answer is, certainly not! If he does believe in reincarnation, it would be a mistake for him to renounce the belief unless his internal Teacher so advised. And this is most unlikely." (5:1-3)

"All that must be recognized, however, is that birth was not the beginning, and death is not the end." (5:7)

"The emphasis of this course always remains the same;- it is at this moment that complete salvation is offered you, and it is at this moment you can accept it. This is still your one responsibility." (6:1-2)

"Heaven is here. There is no other time." (6:6-7)

ME: I suppose that makes sense. I hold no grievances against whomever had to abort me. I am completely unharmed. And according to You, I still love this person very much. Can I ask who I volunteered to do this for? Do I know them now?

HS: Yes, you know them in this dream. However, I will not reveal their identity to you at this time. This person will one day read this book, and if they read it here that they once aborted you, they would feel intense guilt over this. They love you as much as you love them. Even if you left their name out here,

I would not have your loved ones asking you who it was. It does not matter. What matters is, the lesson was learned; the situation is over. No one was harmed. It is never My purpose to increase guilt, and so I will not reveal their identity. I only take guilt away.

ME: Yeah, I forget that a lot. My only excuse is that I'm operating on just 10% of my brain capacity. Speaking of our brains, is it true that we don't use our whole brains? What's all the extra space for anyway?

HS: Where do you think your eternal memories are stored once they are returned to you?

ME: Good grief, *that's* what all our untapped brainpower is for?

HS: Yes. When you use an MRI device to scan for brain activity, it lights up in the areas that are active. Normally, this type of scan will show shifts and changes in light as you use different parts of your brain. If you could've done an MRI on Christ when He walked the world as the man Jesus, His mind would've shown up as one solid, unchanging light. His brain was fully *enlightened*. His thoughts did not shift or change; there was just one light, one Thought: God's Thought of Unity. He remembered everything about Who He Was, and this filled every portion of His mind with light. If you regain the memory of Who You Are while still within your bodily form, this is the change you would experience. You would then be able to raise the dead, cure the blind and literally move mountains; exactly as Jesus could; all with the God given power of your mind. Please insert the quote from the Course explaining this.

The following quotations from the Course are from TEXT Chapter 2 — VI. Fear and Conflict

"Few appreciate the real power of the mind, and no one remains fully aware of it all the time." (9:3)

"The mind is very powerful, and never loses its creative force. It never sleeps. Every instant it is creating. It is hard to recognize that thought and belief combine into a power surge that can literally move mountains. It appears at first glance that to believe such power about yourself is arrogant, but that is not the real reason you do not believe it. You prefer to believe that your thoughts cannot exert real influence because you are actually afraid of them." (9:5-10)

"There *are* no idle thoughts. All thinking produces form at some level." (9:13-14)

ME: Holy crap. That's incredible! I guess I really need to purify my thoughts then if I want full use of my brain.

HS: It's not so much *full* use as *proper* use. Ego thoughts produce changes in emotional states and conflict, but thoughts inspired by Me produce unchanging joy and happiness. Purifying your thoughts to this level is a good idea.

ME: All that power sounds kind of dangerous though. Even after our thoughts are purified.

HS: Do not let the power of your own thoughts cause you fear, because it is this very fear that limits them. Just as you do not give your children matches, scissors, or knives to play with until they are old enough to be responsible with them, you are not allowed a power that would truly cause you harm. There is a built in "safety mechanism" to ensure no real harm can come to you before you fully understand your true capabilities. This illusion is a place where you can safely play with seemingly dangerous toys without causing yourself real harm. Now it is time to put away your childish toys and know your full power in My Name. I believe you know the quote I would like here. It is the explanation of how you "fell asleep" and you temporarily gave up all your power to create with Me.

The following quotations from the Course are from TEXT Chapter 29 — IX. The Forgiving Dream

"Hear, then, your story in the dream you made, and ask yourself if it be not the truth that you believe that it is not a dream." (1:4)

"A dream of judgement came into the mind that God created

perfect as Himself. And in that dream was Heaven changed to hell, and God made enemy unto His Son. How can God's Son awaken from the dream? It is a dream of judgment. So must he judge not, and he will waken. For the dream will seem to last while he is part of it." (2:1-5)

"All figures in the dream are idols, made to save you from the dream. Yet they are part of what they have been made to save you *from*. Thus does an idol keep the dream alive and terrible, for who could wish for one unless he were in terror and despair?" (3:1-3)

"There can be no salvation in the dream as you are dreaming it." (4:1)

"Little child, the light is there. You do but dream, and idols are the toys you dream you play with. Who has need of toys but children? They pretend they rule the world, and give their toys the power to move about, and talk and think and feel and speak for them. Yet everything their toys appear to do is in the minds of those who play with them." (4:3-7)

"Nightmares are childish dreams. They toys have turned against the child who thought he made them real. Yet can a dream attack?" (5:1-3)

"There is a time when childhood should be passed and gone forever. Seek not to retain the toys of children. Put them all away, for you have need of them no more. The dream of judgment is a children's game, in which the child become the father, powerful, but with the little wisdom of a child." (6:1-4)

"Whenever you feel fear in any form,- and you *are* fearful if you do not feel a deep content, a certainty of help, a calm assurance Heaven goes with you,- be sure you made an idol, and believe it will betray you." (9:1)

"Forgiving dreams remind you that you live in safety and have not attacked yourself. So do your childish terrors melt away, and dreams become a sign that you have made a new beginning, not another try to worship idols and to keep attack. Forgiving dreams are kind to everyone who figures in the dream. And so they bring the dreamer full release from dreams of fear." (10:1-4)

ME: In other words, I need to put away my childish thoughts that I am a body and can be harmed and cause harm. Through forgiving and blessing the world instead of judging it as though it is real, I exercise my new "adult" view of the world, thus releasing myself from my own dream.

HS: You are correct. No one can fully awaken from the dream *until you see Me in all things.* You must know that all living things echo My Voice.

Chapter 14: Lessons 151-170

Forgiving the Good and Bad Together

151. All things are echoes of the Voice for God.

HS: To hear an echo, you must be completely quiet, and listen very carefully. All other sounds must be hushed. This is how My Voice within you is heard. I speak to you behind all your loud thoughts of fear about this world; just like a faint echo. *All things are echoes of the Voice for God.* To hear My Voice behind all things, you must decide forgive all things their physical form and see only My Light within them. The power to decide this is your own.

152. The power of decision is my own.

HS: The power to decide to quietly forgive this world, is your own. Humbly accept the truth about yourself and all living things; you are perfect, just as God created you. Decide to claim your power now. *The power of decision is your own.* Set aside all other self concepts, and accept only what God's Will created you to be. You are God's Son, and you are Love. To think you are anything less, is a defense against the truth of Who You Really Are. Let down your defenses.

153. In my defenselessness my safety lies.

HS: In this world, the thought of being defenseless brings fear to your heart. You feel someone may "get by" with hurting you if do not defend yourself. In Heaven, you see yourself as having nothing to defend *against. In your defenselessness your safety lies.* You are wholly safe and whole within your Father God. You are One, and there is nothing against which you must defend yourself. *All* is included in the Whole. You are safe among His ministers, Who are created One with you.

154. I am among the ministers of God.

HS: Accept your role as God's holy messenger. He knows Who You Really Are, and He has called you to be His minister. *You are among the minsters of God.* You did not write the message, nor do you decide to whom it should be given. He will send you those who are ready to learn it, and guide you in what to say. Step back from what you decide alone, and let God lead the way.

155. I will step back and let Him lead the way.

HS: You must learn to step back from your ego, and allow Me to lead you. *Step back and let God lead the way.* You will know whether it is the ego you follow or God, based upon how you feel. If your peace is disturbed in the least way, you are following your ego. Through forgiveness of these feelings, choose to walk with God in perfect holiness.

156. I walk with God in perfect holiness.

HS: You have walked with your ego in this illusionary place, on thousands of useless journeys. Let this be your last useless journey. Remember Who walks with you in truth. *You walk with God in perfect holiness.* He has never left you. He has walked beside you, in front of you, and within you; all through the ages. And He is with you still. You are in His Presence now.

157. Into His Presence would I enter now.

HS: To enter into His Presence, there is nothing to wait for, nothing to do beforehand. You have never left God, but your awareness of His Presence has been forgotten. *Into His Presence would you enter now.* Sit in silence and reflect deeply on this, giving gratitude and honor to those who journey with you. Pay no attention to the form your brother appears to be in, nor the unloving words he may speak at times. This is all part of the illusion, and has nothing to do with Who They Are In Truth. See only Christ in them, as you would have them see Christ in you. This is a gift you both give and receive.

158. Today I learn to give as I receive.

HS: When you are able to look past the body, you can let go of the roles you've assigned to others. This frees everyone from the chains you bound them to in the illusion. This is a gift to both of you, because as you are released, you release others. *Today you learn to give as you receive.* This is the law of giving. You give a miracle to both yourself and your brother every time you look past the body.

159. I give the miracles I have received.

HS: It is through seeing all people as the light and love that they are, that true vision and your lost eternal memories are restored to you. Give the miracle of forgiveness, in order that you may receive it. *You give the miracles you have received.* Lose all fear of your brothers, and they will show you the way home. Do not fear them as strangers, but see them as long lost friends.

160. I am at home. Fear is the stranger here.

HS: You have never left your true Home in God. It is an impossibility to leave Him, Who *is* your Home. He sustains you, and without Him you would cease to exist. It is *you* who introduced fear, the stranger, to your relationships. You decided to try to separate, which welcomed fear. And now you no longer remember your true Home, and you are lost and afraid indeed. Yet take heart; *you are at home. Fear is the stranger here.* Fear nothing and no one, for they are all God's holy Sons, and give you only blessings.

161. Give me your blessing, holy Son of God.

HS: Your way Home is simple. You are not lost. You will find your way again as you welcome your brothers without attack, without judgment or condemnation. It is through them you welcome the memory of Me, and of Home. Ask Me to step forward and reveal Myself to you in your brothers. This request will never be denied. Perhaps you are not ready to see Me just yet, and perhaps there will be a long delay from the time of your asking and My answer. Know this though; I *will* answer. Ask then, of all your brothers with deepest sincerity; *give me your blessing, holy Son of God.* Underneath the body they remain My holy Son, as I created them.

162. I am as God created me.

HS: If you truly understood that you are as God created you, your world as you know it would be healed instantly. *You are as God created you.* God created you as Perfect Love, because that is what He Is. God cannot create something He is not, and you cannot *be* something you are not. You cannot die, though you seem to be in a body that dies. There is no such thing as death. You are always and forever free.

163. There is no death. The Son of God is free.

HS:　　What is death to the immortal Son of God? What could kill the eternal, the infinite, and the perfect? Nothing can, but it is possible to make an illusion so convincing, so real, that you react to it as though it can. You are like children playing make-believe on a beach with a kingdom made of sandcastles. Yet, you haven't learned that the sandcastles aren't real. Say goodbye to them now as the waves wash them away, knowing the kingdom you built wasn't meant to last. Such is the nature of this world and your bodies. You are playing one big game of make-believe. How many lifetimes will it take to learn this? In truth, *there is no death. The Son of God is free*. You have never left Him Who is your Source.

164. Now are we one with Him Who is our Source.

HS:　　There is no time but the eternal moment of *now*. There is no other "time" that is real. The past is gone, and the future is yet to be. *Now are you one with Him Who is your Source*. He is always present in you, because you are literally a Thought within His Mind.

165. Let not my mind deny the Thought of God.

HS:　　Each one of you is a unique Loving Thought of God. He thought of you, and this brought you into being. When you deny knowing your brothers as such, you believe they are a body; you deny that they are God's Thought. *Let not your mind deny the Thought of God*. Love your brothers as they are in truth; each one, a loving Thought of God. This is the gift you are entrusted to give them.

166. I am entrusted with the gifts of God.

HS:　　Loving your brothers as God created them is the greatest gift you can give. Giving this gift must be practiced, because you still do not believe it. Treat each brother with the love and honor that is their due. This is the gift God has entrusted you with. *You are entrusted with the gifts of God*. You are all part of one life, and share it with God.

167. There is one life, and that I share with God.

HS:　　You cannot leave your Source. *There is one life, and that you share with God.* As you see your union instead of your differences, your Divinity is reflected back to you through your brothers. You are given the grace of God. It is yours to claim.

168. Your grace is given me. I claim it now.

HS:　What is grace, but the state of loving in a loveless place? *His grace is given you. Claim it now.* His Love has gone nowhere. You have only looked away. Live His grace through loving one another as He loves you, and you will be released.

169. By grace I live. By grace I am released.

HS:　Grace will carry you past this world entirely. Yet, grace cannot come to a mind that is not receptive to it. You prepare your mind through forgiveness. Practice forgiveness in every moment. Release your brothers of all you think they are. Live as though you already believe you are One. This is living in grace, and the means by which you will release yourself. *By grace you live. By grace are you released.* Love all people, because no one you see is cruel in truth. God cannot create what is unlike Himself.

170. There is no cruelty in God and none in me.

HS:　You see each other through fear. You react in defense or attack towards one another daily; even slight irritation is a form of attack. Cruelty in any form, is actually a cry for help; a desperate plea for release from pain through love. You will know you no longer believe in cruelty, when you cease to see it in yourself and your brothers, and extend only love. Whenever you feel angry, afraid, or even slightly irritated, remember the truth about yourselves; *there is no cruelty in God and none in you.*

· · ·

ME:　So, if I'm understanding this correctly, we are supposed to forgive all that we see with our bodily eyes; especially the bodies we see. We are not to believe any of it is real, because we can't see our true reality with our bodily eyes, much less the Christ within one another. So we need to practice forgiveness of it. A lot. We do this by not believing what we see, knowing it is a mistake. Forgiveness will release us from this reality, bringing our awareness to Heaven. And we can do all this without leaving our bodies?

HS: Correct. You do not have to leave your body until you are finished with it.

ME: How do I know when I'm done with it, if I'm continually trying to deny that it is me? What if I wanted to leave it right now?

HS: You are done living in a body, whence your forgiveness lessons are complete; when you no longer hold a grievance against anyone. Your heart must come into total peace, and remain there. Until then, you are destined to return here again and again, seeking what you will not find.

ME: Buuuuh. That sounds like it will take me forever. I'm not so sure this is my last life. I mean, it seems so unfair! This world feels so real. I don't think it's possible for me to see past it. Especially the people. I can't help but feel like You should intervene somehow, knowing that deep down, we all just want to stop suffering and come Home. Forgiveness of the world seems unattainable to me.

HS: This is why the Course calls forgiveness a *miracle*. If it were easy, it'd be called something else.

ME: Ha ha.

HS: I believe you know the quote I would like you to place here next.

ME: Yep. I'm on it.

The following quotations from the Course are from TEXT Chapter 24 — III. The Forgiveness of Specialness

"Forgiveness is the end of specialness. Only illusions can be forgiven, and then they disappear." (1:1-2)

"Whatever form of specialness you cherish, you have made sin." (2:1)

"It is not *you* who are so vulnerable and open to attack that just a word, a little whisper that you do not like, a circumstance that suits you not, or an event that you did not anticipate upsets your world, and hurls it into chaos. Truth is not frail." (3:1-2)

"God asks for your forgiveness. He would have no separation, like an alien will, rise between what He wills for you and what you will." (5:1-2)

"And God Himself, Who knows that death is not your will, must say, "Thy will be done" because you think it is." (5:8)

"Forgive the great Creator of the universe, the Source of life, of love and holiness, the perfect Father of a perfect Son, for your illusions of your specialness. Here is the hell you chose to be your home. He chose not this for you." (6:1-3)

"Yet if you would release your brother from the depths of hell, you have forgiven Him Whose Will it is you rest forever in the arms of peace, in perfect safety, and without the heat and malice of one thought of specialness to mar your rest." (6:6)

"The special ones are all asleep, surrounded by a world of loveliness they do not see." (7:1)

"Open your eyes a little; see the savior God gave to you that you might look on him, and give him back his birthright. It is yours." (7:7-8)

"The slaves of specialness will yet be free. Such is the Will of God and of His Son." (8:1-2)

"God asks your mercy on His Son and on Himself." (8:7)

"They seek your love that you may love yourself. Love not your specialness instead of Them. The print of nails is on your hands as well. Forgive your Father it was not His Will that you be crucified." (8:10-13)

ME: Hm. This is a long one. But overall I think it means that we're still choosing to be here as long as we desire to be "special" somehow? That perhaps we think we're better than others or that some are more deserving of Your Love than others?

HS: Yes. You asked God to grant you specialness in His love, but that was the one thing He could not give. He loves you all equally in His Sonship, and it is impossible for Him to love anyone more or less than another. Until you accept that, you must return here again and again. It is the belief you can be something separate, more, or apart that holds you here in the dream.

ME: You make it sound as though I should feel guilty for liking anything here. I mean, I feel as though I shouldn't enjoy any of it, because we made it in error. You even call all this error "sin," which makes me feel even worse. What about all the *good* stuff? I don't like the idea of giving up sunsets, and ice cream. I also enjoy riding my horses in the woods, and making love to my husband (not at the same time of course). Is all of that sinful? Am I supposed to suddenly give it all up, because liking it is keeping me here in the illusion? I don't want to stop having fun and live like a pious prude.

HS: Forgiveness asks no sacrifice of you. In fact, forgiveness asks just the opposite. The more you forgive the world around you, releasing the Son of God within each body, the easier your life becomes. Then you will enjoy it much more when you know you have nothing to lose. Do not give up anything that brings you joy and happiness, but neither should you covet it. Sacrifice only that which causes you pain, and enjoy the rest; knowing it is only temporary. See everything as simply nothing; even making love to your husband.

ME: Nice, I'll tell him all sex is meaningless. He'll like that. Anyway, so You're saying we should love all things and people without special attachment; knowing this is all an illusion. Like watching a movie?

HS: Yes, but most importantly, let go of the past you see in your brother. See him only as he is in the present moment. Then life is transformed into a happier dream. You will notice an increase in positive "coincidences" as you practice forgiveness with increasing frequency. Things will begin to "go your way," but it cannot be *you* who dictates the way. Accept all things as they come to you without resistance. Allow nothing to disturb your peace, as you remember that everything is a forgiveness lesson you must learn; both the "bad" and the "good." The lessons will get easier as you go along. Difficult forgiveness lessons may be removed from your future as you let go of present grievances.

ME: How so?

HS: We will discuss that at the end of the next chapter. It all rests on trust. Trust in your brothers, and trust in Me.

ME: Well that's just the problem. I don't trust a lot of the people out there. What if they read this, then decide that doing bad things to other people gives them happiness? What if they think, "I can rob, rape, and abuse whomever I want. No big deal. None of this is real anyway. I'll just forgive it when I'm done."

HS: Forgiveness is to see another person as part of yourself, and if that is being truly practiced, you would not want to harm another human being. Ever. Forgiveness does no harm. It does not increase guilt, pain, or suffering in yourself or another. It is total peace. If someone were to have such compulsions to do harm, it would only mean they were deeply embedded within the ego and the dream. Impulses to do harm to yourself and others naturally fades away as true forgiveness is practiced.

ME: Oh, so instead of fearing them, I need to practice trusting that You are within all those people; knowing that You are helping each of us with the appropriate forgiveness lessons?

HS: Correct. If someone is increasing fear and discomfort in any form within you, you must see them only with forgiveness. It may be necessary to leave their presence though, if you are unable to feel love and peace towards them in a given situation. It is okay to simply forgive yourself for being unable to forgive at the time. During those times, there may be no other choice than to physically remove yourself from the situation. Do not fear. Peace will be found. Do your best. Trust in your Oneness with them and Me, and trust in the the lessons they each present to you. It may be your lesson in having the strength and courage to leave them.

ME: I see then that You don't expect us to just lie down and take abuse. I wonder though, why didn't Jesus just leave instead of allowing Himself to be abused and crucified?

HS: He allowed it only to demonstrate that He was not a body, He was free. It was not His death that freed you, but His resurrection. His message wasn't that it was a sacrifice to die for you. His intended message was that He loved you so much, that He was willing to allow you to "kill" Him in order to demonstrate He was *not* a body and cannot be killed. He wanted you to believe this through seeing Him lay down His bodily life without hesitation, and rise again. He then bestowed Himself upon you all, in the form of Me, the Holy Spirit.

ME: Wait. So am I actually talking to Jesus or the Holy Spirit here?

HS: I am the Holy Spirit; His Spokesperson. The Voice of God and Christ. You are talking to Me, Who is One with Them, and when you speak with Me, you speak directly with Them. When Christ poured out His Spirit onto the flesh of all mankind, He became One with you. This was His gift to humanity. He is within all of you, waiting to be recognized by you for the second time, in one another. It is God's Will that you cease attempting to crucify Him by hating each other. Love one another as He loves you. Hear My Voice within you, calling you to trust in your brothers who are one with you.

Chapter 15: Lessons 181-200

Forgiveness Makes Life Easier

181. I trust my brothers, who are one with me.

HS: To fully trust, means that you have laid aside all your defenses. Trust requires you to be totally without fear. *Trust your brothers, who are one with you.* If you feel anger or any form of fear, you are not trusting in the holiness within your brothers. You have forgotten they contain Christ and are one with you. Forgive this, and move back into peace. Peace and stillness are your natural state of Being. It is through practicing inner stillness in the face of adversity that you learn the way home.

182. I will be still an instant and go home.

HS: You all have an inner restlessness, an ongoing anxiety, depression, or a subtle feeling of "unrest." You are continually searching for something to alleviate this restlessness; be it more money, a lover, a job, a home, or an addiction. You don't recognize what you are really searching for. You are actually searching for Home. *Be still an instant and go home.* You have only to call on My Name, and I will lead you there.

183. I call upon God's Name and on my own.

HS: The Name of God is beyond all form, beyond all words. God Is. His Name is an *experience* you seek. His Name is the awakening to your Unity. No one is exempt from God's Name. Your ability to see the world through Christ's eyes is to remember your Total Union. To do this, *call upon God's Name and your own,* which is to ask for total peace in His Union. This peace is your inheritance.

184. The Name of God is my inheritance.

HS: As God's Son, you naturally inherit His Name. *The Name of God is your inheritance.* A son inherits from his father, and God your Father has passed on all that He is, to you. You have merely forgotten that this is so. It is a state of Being One. It is the peace of God. Deep down, you know His peace is all you want.

185. I want the peace of God.

HS: To attain total peace, your mind must be completely healed of the illusion of separation. There is not a single person on this planet experiencing the illusion right now, who doesn't want peace. *You want the peace of God.* To achieve this, you must look within yourself at every uncomfortable feeling, every twinge of dissatisfaction. Why are you feeling this way? What part of the illusion is making you unhappy? Maybe you can determine a specific cause and maybe you can't. Don't waste your time thinking about it. All discomfort will eventually trace back to your original feeling of guilt for having chosen to forget Me. This is the only thing you need to forgive, and all else will be healed. This will bring salvation to the world, and it depends on you.

186. Salvation of the world depends on me.

HS: The world is saved from all illusion when you accept at last that you are God's Son and not a body. *Salvation of the world depends on you.* Whenever you respond to the dream as though it's real; whenever you feel discomfort or pain; whenever *any* emotion crops up that isn't peace; you must forgive it immediately. Most of you do not feel peace, most of the time. You must reverse your thinking by blessing every tiny discomfort with forgiveness. By doing this, you bless the world and you bless yourself.

187. I bless the world because I bless myself.

HS: A blessing is a forgiveness, and to forgive is a miracle. A miracle is a healing. You are all here to become miracle workers, and miracles are wrought through the extension of your Love to one another. *You bless the world because you bless yourself.* It is a miracle to see past the illusion to the peace of God that is shining in you now.

188. The peace of God is shining in me now.

HS: The peace of God has never left you. It is part of Who You Are. The peace of God is woven into the very fabric of your being. You cannot lose it, but you can choose not to feel it. *The peace of God is shining in you now.* To awaken to this fact, you must un-choose who you think you are. Know that you are God's Son. Feel His love within you now.

189. I feel the Love of God within me now.

HS: What you see outside of you, stems from what you feel within. This is the Law of Seeing. If you feel peace and love, you will see a world of peace and love. If you feel fear and hate, you will see a world of fear and hate. This is how you manifest your experience within the dream. You can change your experience by forgiving all feelings that are not love. *Feel the Love of God within you now.* Choose the joy of God instead of pain.

190. I choose the joy of God instead of pain.

HS: Pain is witness to the ego. *Choose the joy of God instead of pain.* Choose joy above all other thoughts. Have no other idle wishes that project anything other than joy. This world does not hold you prisoner, it is prisoner to your thinking. You have the power to heal the world through your very thoughts. This is your power, and it comes from God, because you are the holy Son of God Himself.

191. I am the holy Son of God Himself.

HS: Believe this one thought and you set the world free. *You are the holy Son of God Himself.* This thought corrects your self perception and recognizes the truth. It is your declaration of freedom from the world. Deny no longer Your Identity as God's Son. Let this thought replace all other thoughts of this world. When you remember to undo pain with this thought, this choice, this forgiveness; a miracle is born. All the power in Heaven is given you to work miracles. This is the only function God would have you fill.

192. I have a function God would have me fill. *truly helpful*

HS: It is your function to forgive everything and everyone in this world, including yourself. This is your *only* job. *You have a function God would have you fill.* Forgiveness is what you use to wipe the slate clean and make room for God. Be it forgiveness of a small irritating thought or a huge angry thought; be it a "good thing" or a "bad thing;" it's all the same dream you are forgiving. No forgiveness should be more difficult than another because it's all equally part of the dream. Forgive it all, no matter how big or how small. All things are forgiveness lessons God would have you learn.

193. All things are lessons God would have me learn.

HS: The lessons you receive may each appear to be different, but I assure you, they are all the same. *All things are lessons God would have you learn.* Anything that causes even the tiniest twinge of discomfort is an un-forgiveness needing to be forgiven. This sensation is your built in alarm system. It tells you you've made an error; that you think this illusion real. Learn to see all obstacles to your peace as blessings, leading you closer to God. There may be thousands of disturbances to your peace every single day. Forgive them all, and trust that I am bringing you what is appropriate. Place your future in My Hands.

194. I place the future in the Hands of God.

HS: Your faith and trust in God must rise to such heights that you are wholly without fear. *Place the future in the Hands of God.* To forgive is to let go of your control over outcomes. To forgive is to be okay with whatever is happening to you right now, knowing it was sent by Me, to provide you with a lesson in forgiveness. Faith is simply the practice of serial forgivenesses. Your mind must rest with gratitude and love on everything you encounter. Love is the way you walk in gratitude.

195. Love is the way I walk in gratitude.

HS: In this illusion, you are only grateful for what you have in comparison to others. If you have money, love or health, you feel grateful because it appears others do *not* have these things. Sometimes you feel guilty for having more. Sometimes you feel cheated for having less. Either way, it will never be right because dreams are fickle. And so it will always be, because no dream is real. Be thankful for this! Be glad the world you made is not real, and walk through it lovingly. *Love is the way you walk in gratitude.* Have gratitude that all people are equally loved by God. Be grateful that no one can truly hurt you. You can only crucify yourself.

196. It can be but myself I crucify.

HS: The ego does not want to be at fault for any of your pain. Yet, know the source of your pain is yourself. *It can be but yourself you crucify.* Accept this. But then also accept that you are not an ego, and that God is your Father and you are His Son. This thought is the one correction for all other thoughts. Through this thought, you gratefully heal yourself. It can be but your own gratitude you earn.

197. It can be but my gratitude I earn.

HS: Sometimes, it may appear that nothing has happened when you forgive, or things seem to get even worse. And often, you will not see gratitude in exchange for your forgivenesses, because it is an unseen act. Rest assured, your forgiveness is always received, even if it seems to have no immediate healing effect. Results are not always apparent on the level of form, but results *always* manifest in the realm of Spirit. It is in Heaven that the greatest changes are happening, even if they do not materialize in form on earth. You will thank yourself later for your forgivenesses now. When you forgive, you must always remember the forgiveness will come back to you because you are One. *It can be but your gratitude you earn.* And likewise, only your condemnation injures you.

198. Only my condemnation injures me.

HS: You only hurt yourself through your thoughts about what you believe. Change your beliefs, and you change your experience of the illusion. What you feel, is what you see. Why not release all condemnation and forgive? Forgiveness undoes all forms of pain. *Only your condemnation injures you.* Once all lessons in forgiveness have been learned, there will be nothing within but peace. Out of the silence of this peace, you will remember you are not a body, you are free.

199. I am not a body. I am free.

HS: Your body is home of the ego and it will not let go of this idea gently, because it knows it will cease to exist once you accept you are God's Son. Let go of your white knuckled grip on outcomes in the world, and know it is all part of the illusion, designed to keep you fixated on problems outside yourself. *You are not a body. You are free.* Through your Unity in Spirit you are free, and through your separation you are slave to the ego. Once you accept the gift of your freedom in God, you will experience His peace. And there is no peace except the peace of God.

200. There is no peace except the peace of God.

HS: The peace of God is the final goal you have, whether you're openly aware of it or not. You seek the level of happiness and satisfaction only God's peace can bring. *There is no peace except the peace of God.* You will not find this peace out in the world. It cannot be found by *denying* any comforts you find in the world either. God asks for no sacrifices. His Will is not your further suffering. It is okay to enjoy all the world has to offer you, but do not be deceived into thinking it is real. Forgive it and forget it.

· · ·

ME: So, You said in the previous chapter that forgiveness lessons can be lessened or removed from our future. What do You mean by that? And how is this accomplished?

HS: As stated in the lessons above, forgiveness of the illusion undoes it. During the "undoing" process, the dream will shift to a happier one for you. As you practice forgiveness of the world, everything will begin to slide into harmony around you. Painful lessons that you initially "asked" for, may be removed or greatly lessened, as you will no longer need them to bring you closer to Me. Forgiveness is a demonstration of your willingness to see things differently, and a lack of resistance to All That Is, which causes your life to flow down an easier path. You will see immediate results, and these results will hasten and encourage you to practice further forgiveness.

ME: I believe I have an example of when this noticeably happened to me. You directly intervened when a snowboarding "accident" could've injured me permanently.

HS: Yes. My interventions are not always so obvious, but I would like you to briefly describe that event now.

ME: Alright.

Back in February of 2014, my husband and I decided to take a five day snowboarding trip out to Big Sky Montana. During our time there, we discovered a rather difficult ski run called "Challenger Peak."

It was truly a challenging peak. There were signs at the bottom of the chair lift warning skiers and snowboarders it was for experts only due to the large rocks, constant high winds and blinding snow at the top; which consisted of a narrow ledge with an immediate near vertical drop.

On the final morning of our stay there, I awoke at 4:00 a.m. to an inner message from You; instructing me that Paul and I should not go up to that particular peak on our final day. You told me that I would sustain permanent injuries to both my left hip and knee.

I didn't tell Paul about Your message right away. I wanted to see how things would play out on their own, despite my worry he would want to go up there on our last day. However, You even took care of that point. When we stopped for a break, and noticed we were actually at the base of Challenger Peak (which would've been a huge short cut to where we were headed) Paul uncharacteristically decided to stay on the longer, easier route. At the end of the day, we returned to our room, "accident free."

I have a few questions about why You did this. I mean, why was I spared this injury?

HS: Because you had progressed far enough along in your forgiveness lessons at that point, the experience was no longer necessary. It had been removed from your future. By then, you were no longer asking for that degree of bodily suffering. You no longer needed to experience that level of physical pain in order to learn certain forgiveness lessons you had already decided upon before incarnating here.

ME: But I had only progressed six months into my first time through the 365 lessons from the Course. How could so short a time make such a difference? I hadn't even really begun to understand what I was supposed to be doing yet. What does *forgiveness* have to do with certain lessons or events being removed from my life?

HS: You can reduce much suffering for yourself when you remember to forgive. It was due to forgiveness lessons you are accomplishing now, that affected changes in your past. Each forgiveness is a miracle. Miracle Principle 13 clearly states how this is possible:

> *"Miracles are both beginnings and endings, and so they alter the temporal order. They are always affirmations of rebirth, which seem to go back but really go forward. They undo the past in the present, and thus release the future."* (TEXT-I.I.13:1-3 Miracle Principle 13)

ME: I don't understand this so clearly yet. Please continue to explain.

HS: You "un-ask" for certain lessons through forgiveness of what you see in this world. Through denying its reality, you undo its power to affect you. True forgiveness is seeing the world and all living things in it as part of you. To look upon the world in this way, is acceptance of the Atonement. It is through the Atonement that all things are healed and made whole once again. My Word is that you are One. Accept this, and miracles flow into your life in a very real way. And when you accept My Word, you demonstrate you are a true teacher of God.

The following quotations from the Course are from
MANUAL FOR TEACHERS
22. How Are Healing and Atonement Related?

"Healing and Atonement are not related; they are identical." (1:1)

"Accept Atonement and you are healed. Atonement is the Word of God. Accept His Word and what remains to make sickness possible? Accept His Word and every miracle has been accomplished. To forgive is to heal. The teacher of God has taken accepting the atonement for himself as his only function." (1:5-10)

"The progress of the teacher of God may be slow or rapid, depending on whether he recognizes the Atonement's inclusiveness, or for a time excludes some problem areas from it. In some cases, there is a sudden and complete awareness of the perfect applicability of the lesson of the Atonement to all situations, but this is comparatively rare. The teacher of God may have accepted the function God has given him long before he has learned all that his acceptance holds out to him. It is only the end that is certain. Anywhere along the way, the necessary realization of inclusiveness may reach him. If the way seems long, let him be content. He has decided on the direction he wants to take. What more was asked of him? And having done what was required, would God withhold the rest?" (2:1-9)

"That forgiveness is healing needs to be understood, if the teacher of God is to make progress. The idea that the body can be sick is a central concept in the ego's thought system." (3:1-2)

"Certainly sickness does not appear to be a decision. Nor would anyone actually believe he wants to be sick. Perhaps he can accept the idea in theory, but it is rarely if ever consistently applied to all specific forms of sickness, both in the individual's perception of himself and of all others as well. Nor is it at this level that the teacher of God calls forth the miracle of healing. He overlooks the mind *and* body, seeing only the face of Christ shining in front of him, correcting all mistakes and healing all perception." (4:1-5)

"When a teacher of God fails to heal, it is because he has forgotten Who he is." (5:1)

"Step back now, teacher of God. You have been wrong. Lead not the way, for you have lost it. Turn quickly to your Teacher, and let yourself be healed." (5:7-10)

"The offer of Atonement is universal. It is equally applicable to all individuals in all circumstances. And in it is the power to heal all individuals of all forms of sickness." (6:1-3)

"It is your task to heal the sense of separation that has made him sick. It is your function to recognize for him that what he believes about himself is not the truth. It is your forgiveness that must show him this. Healing is very simple. Atonement is received and offered." (6:7-11)

"Herein does he receive Atonement, for he withdraws his judgment from the Son of God, accepting him as God created him. No longer does he stand apart from God, determining where healing should be given and where it should be withheld. Now can he say with God, "This is my beloved Son, created perfect and forever so." (7:8-10)

HS: Remember what true forgiveness *is*. It is the undoing of fear. The undoing of your sense of separation from Me and each other. This world arose out of the illusion of your fear and separation from Me and every time you forgive, you are undoing part of that illusion, and with it, some of the coinciding unpleasant experiences. You choose to experience seemingly "bad" things in order to provide yourself with the opportunities you need to practice forgiveness, and thus overcome all fear and return your mind to a state of peace and love.

"Miracles represent freedom from fear. "Atoning" means "undoing." The undoing of fear is an essential part of the Atonement value of miracles." (TEXT-1.I.26:1-3 Miracle Principle 26)

HS: Typically, lessons are removed or reduced subtly and unbeknownst to you. You cannot avoid all your forgiveness lessons entirely though. Sometimes they must be endured because it is the most efficient way for you to learn. These hard times may not feel pleasant in the moment, but the payoff is tremendous in the realm of Spirit. Always rejoice in your suffering with deepest gratitude. Everything is for your benefit. It is through true forgiveness; the understanding that what you see with your bodily eyes is not real; that you induce miracles to remove painful lessons from your life.

ME: Interesting. You know, my life seems pretty good to me. I mean, I feel as though I haven't suffered very much compared to some people.

Compared to a *lot* of people actually. Does an easy life indicate how spiritually advanced a person is?

HS: Absolutely not. Jesus was the most spiritually advanced person to walk the earth, and yet He outwardly appeared to endure much suffering at times in His life. You cannot know or judge how far another is on their spiritual path, based on their life circumstances.

ME: How do we know how far along we are on our path then?

HS: There is no distance you need to cover on your path, because you have never left Me to begin with. My path is forever beneath your feet. It is only your *awareness* of this that needs to be restored. This can be accomplished at *any* time. However, removing the barriers to this memory may seem to take time while you remain within the framework of time. Some people decide to save their most difficult barriers for their last life, while others may decide to complete the most challenging earlier. Either way, everyone is here to perform their function of forgiveness. Big or small, you're here to forgive it all. Jesus completed everything in a single trip. His life was sweet, difficult, and supremely beautiful. He lived every moment with perfect forgiveness and in this way, He lived a perfect life.

ME: Oh, so we should just know that whatever we're going through at this moment is something we need to forgive, and not worry about how much work we have left to do? That really goes against my nature. I like knowing how my progress is coming along.

HS: No matter how "good" or "bad" a life may seem, it is no indication of progress. However, through forgiveness, the same problems will cease to crop up for you again and again. The degree or nature of the problem doesn't matter, and whether a person's life is easy or hard is not an indication of spiritual advancement. Someone living on the streets or who has a terrible drug addiction could be living their last life here, or a person living a life of seeming ease and comfort may be only just beginning.

ME: Is there no obvious way to gauge our spiritual progress then?

HS: If you truly want to know how spiritually advanced you are, just look at how loving you are towards others. The degree to which you consistently and *sincerely* display love, kindness, and affection towards all those you see, under every circumstance, is the degree to which you are spiritually advanced.

ME: Oh. I see.

HS: And just as you should not judge how far another has come along on their path of forgiveness, neither should you judge their spiritual beliefs. If ever you feel the burning need to correct someone in their spiritual belief or practice, then do it My Way. Allow them to be just as they are, and love them just as I do. *Always be the example of My Love.* All people are at varying stages of faith and growth, and all will be lead to Me at the right time. As to when that time is, is not your problem. However, that time can be hastened for yourself through learning to accept peace into your mind. You do this by letting all your thoughts about the world be still.

Chapter 16: Lessons 221-230

What Is The World For Anyway?

221. Peace to my mind. Let all my thoughts be still.

HS: Through forgiveness you come to your Father and show faith that He will come to you. Your silence within says that you are ready for Him. Be patient. Be still. Never forget that God is with you, and you live and move in Him.

222. God is with me. I live and move in Him.

HS: God provides you with all you need. Your body may have endless needs, but you are not a body. You are joined in holy union with God and He delivers you from all that the body seems to demand. Be still and quiet within, and forgive what you are not; sit in peaceful wonder of all that You Really Are. God is with you, right now; He is your life and you have no life but His.

223. God is my life. I have no life but His.

HS: This is the most difficult thing for your ego to hear. The ego would have you believe this world is your real home, and that your life appears to depend on *it*. Your true Home and true Life is in God, and He is *within* you. He gives you life, because He is your Father, and unlike the ego, your Father God loves you, His Son.

224. God is my Father, and He loves His Son.

HS: This world obscures the truth in every way. Nowhere out in the world will you find "proof" of your Sonship in God. In fact, the world strives to show you just the opposite. The world shows you a god who is uncaring and merciless. Yet, the world can be used to point the way to Me. You can choose to forgive the world you see, thus allowing Me to restore your memory of Him; the memory that God is your Father, and you love Him.

225. God is my Father, and His Son loves Him.

HS: Your ego quakes at the thought of you remembering your love for God!

119

The ego knows that once you do, you will instantly abandon it. Forgive all the ego has made outside of you and seek only the stillness that lies within. Forgiveness clears the alter within your mind of all cluttered thoughts, thus inviting My Peace, and the memory of your true Home. Your Home awaits You. Hasten there.

226. My home awaits me. I will hasten there.

HS: Why would you desire a reality that only brings you pain? Why would you delay experiencing Heaven a second longer? This world is not your home. But you can ease your journey through it, by forgiving it. You can let go of the world *now*, and experience Heaven immediately. You need not wait a second longer. This is your holy instant of release.

227. This is my holy instant of release.

HS: You are held in bondage to this world by your own choice. You choose it through your unloving and unforgiving thoughts, which in turn, dictate your experience of the world. What you see follows from what you think. What you give is what you receive. You are doing all this to yourself. God is not wreaking revenge and punishment upon you. His Will is only peace and love for you, but you have to *choose* it. Your will must join with His. Do not believe God has condemned you, and neither should you condemn yourself.

228. God has condemned me not. No more do I.

HS: God has not condemned you to suffer in a body. He created you as His Holy Son, in perfect union with each other and Himself. How long before you trust God's Vision of you? How long before you accept His Will? Take it on faith that God's Word is true; you are each a living part of His Sonship. Cease to resist this truth. Understand that Love, which created you, is what you are.

229. Love, which created me, is what I am.

HS: You are Love, because God is Love, and there is nothing else He could use to create you. Welcome the truth of Who You Are, despite the many forms you see around you; whether they appear fearful, ugly, mean, or angry. Do not be fooled. Through remembering this in the present moment, you will seek and find the peace of God.

230. Now will I seek and find the peace of God.

HS: God will not deny you any request for peace. You ask for His peace whenever you forgive that which is *not* peace. Through performing your function of forgiveness, you join with His Will and claim your power in Him. What can stop the power of God? With His Help, you cannot fail to find what you seek.

. . .

ME: I get that we are all here to attain the peace of God, and even though it's been hard to accept, I get the idea that I *chose* to come here, and worse still, that I helped *make* this place somehow. However, it still seems to be beyond my understanding, exactly how I'm expected to transfer my mind over from the ego, to God and His Thoughts. And when that happens, what happens to *me*? Does my personality just disappear into the Oneness? I don't like that idea.

HS: You do not perform the actual function of "mind transfer." That is done by God Himself. You only have to make yourself ready to accept Him-

ME: I know, I know. Through forgiveness. I *got* that. But what I still don't really understand is *how* this is done. How are we One, and yet I'm still *me*? In fact, I've never really understood the whole "Holy Trinity" idea either. You know, how God and Jesus and the Holy Spirit are each seemingly separate people or spirits or whatever, and yet, to know *one* of them, is to know them *all*, because of their Oneness. How is this possible?

(No answer to this question came to me immediately. I waited the rest of the day, but heard only silence from the Voice within me. Then, the next morning, as I opened the Course to read that day's section of TEXT, the answer I sought was found therein):

The following quotations from the Course are from TEXT Chapter 25 — I. The Link to Truth

"Since you believe that you are separate, Heaven presents itself to you as separate, too. Not that it is in truth, but that

the link that has been given you to join the truth may reach to you through what you understand. Father and Son and Holy Spirit are as One, as all your brothers join as one in truth. Christ and His Father never have been separate, and Christ abides within your understanding, in the part of you that shares His Father's Will. The Holy Spirit links the other part- the tiny, mad desire to be separate, different and special- to the Christ, to make the oneness clear to what is really one. In this world this is not understood, but can be taught." (5:1-6)

"The Holy Spirit serves Christ's purpose in your mind, so that the aim of specialness can be corrected where the error lies." (6:1)

"It is the Holy Spirit's function to teach you how this oneness is experienced, what you must do that it can be experienced, and where you should go to do it." (6:4)

"It is apparent that a mind so split could never be the teacher of a Oneness which unites all things within Itself. And so What is within this mind, and does unite all things together, must be its Teacher." (7:2-3)

"All this can very simply be reduced to this:

What is the same can not be different, and what is one can not have separate parts." (7:6-7)

ME: Oh! Got it. I think. Let me see if I've got this right. So even though we look and feel separate, we have to trust that we are one, because oneness cannot be understood while we are here in this world of separation. However, it can be taught to us here, by You, our internal Teacher. We cannot teach it to ourselves, because alone, we only have the ego to listen to- and it only points to what is external. Those who are willing to learn the truth, *will learn it from within.*

HS: Correct. And no, you do not lose your individual personality once your awareness of Oneness is regained. Your personality will retain all that is good and loving- all that is uniquely *you* without the ego. You were made from God's Thought, unique and perfect. This will never be undone, because you are His joy and delight. You will never cease to exist. This is how the Holy Trinity exists. We are each a separate personality, yet joined as One Mind, because We all agree on what is truth. Our Thoughts are One Truth.

ME: Except, being here still seems like a lot of work for nothing, if we're already One with You, and nothing could ever happen to change that fact. *What is the point of anything we see or do?*

HS: A very good question indeed. What *is* the point of anything? I believe you know the quote I'd like here.

The following quotations from the Course are from TEXT Chapter 24 — VII. The Meeting Place

"The test of everything on earth is simply this; *"What is it for?"* The answer makes it what it is for you." (6:1-2)

"Perception seems to teach you what you see. Yet it but witnesses to what you taught. It is the outward picture of a wish; an image that you wanted to be true." (8:8-10)

"Look at yourself, and you will see a body. Look at the body in a different light and it looks different. And without a light it seems that it is gone." (9:1-3)

"Here is an image that you want to be yourself." (9:5)

"And you cannot conceive of you apart from it. You brand it sinful and you hate its acts, judging it evil. Yet your specialness whispers, "Here is my own beloved son, in whom I am well pleased." (10:4-6)

"And thus are two sons made, and both appear to walk this earth without a meeting place and no encounter. One do you perceive outside yourself, your own beloved son. The other rests within, his Father's Son, within your brother as he is in you." (11:1-3)

HS: And so your mind is split between which identity you think you are. On one hand, you desire to be a separate body, ruled by the ego. On the other hand, you are God's holy Son. There is no point to anything you see except to use it to return Home to Me and the memory of your Sonship. Cease to choose to see yourself as a body; the son of the ego, and accept the Son of God within you instead. It is as simple as that. This is all the world is for. You are here to forgive it, and leave it behind. You leave it behind, by joining your will to Mine. My Will is that you remember Me.

Chapter 17: Lessons 231-240

Loving Our Enemies

231. Father, I will but to remember You.

HS: You have no memory of anything prior to your birth. If you did, you would instantly choose to leave here and return to that state of happy bliss and loving awareness of your Sonship in God. It is the memory of this state of satisfied completion that you continue to falsely seek outside yourself in relationships, careers, body obsessions and materialism. Yet, you know from your own experience that a memory has never been found outside of you. Every memory you have, is contained within. Therefore, your lost memory of God is within you as well. Your Father is in your mind, through every day.

232. Be in my mind, my Father, through the day.

HS: God will not barge into your mind by force, because He will not violate your free will. Instead, He will meet you wherever you are, as you open to Him through stillness and peace. As you go about your busy days, remember to apply forgiveness to all things that arise before your eyes. In this way, you release God's stillness upon the world. Give Him your life to guide.

233. I give my life to God to guide today.

HS: Willingly submit everything to God. Give Him everything within your mind that would hinder your salvation. Then watch your life be transformed through forgiveness; becoming peaceful within and without. You don't know who you are or where you are going. You are blind and deaf here within this dream. And so you must put your complete faith and trust in God to guide you safely Home. You must learn once again, that you are His Son.

234. Father, today I am Your Son again.

HS: What does it mean to truly believe this? To have fully accepted your Sonship, is to experience total peace within. If you are in Union, you cannot be at war. If you are peaceful, there can be no conflict. Nothing has ever happened to disturb your peace. You have only dreamed that something has.

Forgive the dream, and know your salvation from it. God in His mercy Wills that you be saved.

235. God in His mercy wills that I be saved.

HS: What does it mean to be saved, except to realize at last, that you have the choice to forgive yourself the mistake of thinking you are separate from God? This is God's Will. In His mercy and love, He keeps the memory of your innocence for you, while you work on remembering your Identity in Him. You are not guilty of any wrongdoing. You have simply forgotten Who You Are. God Wills that you make the choice to awaken and remember this. You rule your own mind, which you alone must rule.

236. I rule my mind, which I alone must rule.

HS: There is no outside force pitted against you. You have total control over what you think and feel. Yet, you spend most of your time blaming outside forces for your problems. You are responsible for how you think and feel about the world. Who will you choose to guide your thoughts? The Holy Spirit or the ego? The choice is yours. Your mind serves you; you do not serve your mind. Turn it over to God, so that you may remember yourself as God created you.

237. Now would I be as God created me.

HS: God created you without conflict. He created you as Unified Love and peace. You are a peace so deep, and so utterly still, that nothing can assail it. To know this, is salvation from the world of conflict. This state has not changed. To know it, is to simply look upon the world and remember it cannot make you separated from each other or your Father. Decide this will be your experience now. It is on your decision all salvation rests.

238. On my decision all salvation rests.

HS: The world you see depends on what you decide, because the world you see is generated by your thoughts. What you feel within, you see without. This power is God's gift to you. What will you do with this powerful gift? You have a choice to make; choose peace and be healed. God loves you so much that He entrusts you with His Power. The glory of your Father is your own.

239. The glory of my Father is my own.

HS: To deny your Sonship, is to reject God's glory. It is true humility to accept at last, your Divine Inheritance. The glory of your Father is yours, because you are created as His Son. No one is excluded from His Sonship, and all seeming separate parts are worthy of His glory. Honor this truth within one another and lay aside all your fears. Because He is within each of you, fear is not justified in any form.

240. Fear is not justified in any form.

HS: All form that exists around you, represents your choice to be separate from Me. It is the choice of fear. Being only temporary from the start, you also fear the loss of such a world. You fear the loss of your job, home, relationships, health, money, body and even the welfare of the entire planet itself. Your fears are not justified. All "matter" does not matter. None of it is eternal, therefore none of it is real. Let go of your attachment to what is temporary, and invest yourself only in what is forever Mine. You are the holy Son of God, and have nothing to fear. You are Love, and Love fears nothing.

. . .

ME: Alright, so we shouldn't fear the loss of anything outside of us, because none of what we see is real; not even our bodies. Right?

HS: Correct. You should only be concerned with what is within, because only that is real; the eternal part of each of you.

ME: And we are all connected as One by this eternal part, so what we do to another, we're actually doing to ourselves. Right?

HS: Correct. I'd like to further clarify this, because for many, it is difficult to see themselves as One with other people. Especially those they despise.

ME: Okay, I'd like to know how I'm supposed to feel compassionate, loving and One with those I despise.

HS: I'm going to tell you something most people find difficult to believe, and almost impossible to accept.

ME: Um. Okay.

HS: I believe you are ready to accept a deeper truth than you currently understand. Ready?

ME: Ready.

HS: *Everyone you see around you, is **you**, in one of your alternate lives.*

ME: Wait. *WHAT*???!!!

Are You saying I've been Hitler? Ivan The Terrible? Murderers? Child molesters? OH MY GOODNESS, I'VE BEEN JUDAS ISCARIOT!!??? I BETRAYED JESUS?!?"

HS: Now you can fully appreciate your amnesia each time you come into this illusion. You wouldn't be able to live your life with all the memories of past lives still in your mind, now would you? There would be no moving forward or accepting that nothing has ever happened to you. Healing would become nearly impossible.

ME: Amnesia or not, how can I *believe* this?! You're right. I *don't* accept it. None of those people are me. I don't see how it can be true.

HS: Well, has knowing this changed anything about you right *now*?

ME: Well... No. I guess not.

HS: Are you still the same person who woke up this morning?

ME: Um... Well yes. I suppose so.

HS: Then okay. Let's just move on. Everything about you, is still *you*, and knowing this doesn't change that. A huge release for you lies in the understanding of this idea, so hang in there. You're still you, but you are also everyone else, living out your other lives. There *is* no one else. Everyone is you, living lives here to work out all aspects of forgiveness. *And everyone else can look at the world from that same perspective.*

Everyone, is everyone else, past, present or future. You are all living out alternate scenarios. You each have an individual part to play, in re-integrating the Whole Sonship. You each have separate personalities, but are still One, working together toward a common goal. Knowing this now, what does it do for your empathy?

ME: Well it changes *everything* for me. I mean, this means that anything I do to someone else, I *literally* do to myself!

HS: Correct. *And this is how you should always see everyone around you.* So the next time you see a morbidly overweight person, a drug addicted person, or anyone else you feel compelled to judge, hate, accuse, or condemn; do *not* condemn or judge them. It is really *you* struggling with addiction and self loathing, or any other problem for that matter; in an alternate life. You are living right there in front of yourself, through everyone else. Now instead of fear and condemnation, try to begin to see through eyes of Christ; Who sees only mercy and forgiveness.

ME: I'm still struggling with accepting this concept. My mind is racing! This means that everyone is screwing this up! *I am screwing this up*! I suddenly want to go around and tell everyone to just stop it!

HS: Let Me reassure you, everything is okay. You are feeling extra guilty right now for everything you think you've done, but I tell you; you are all equally *innocent*. You are all equally you, and you have also been all the *good* people too. There's only one thing you can do to help yourself. Remember, your only job here is to forgive the illusion. Forgive everyone for participating in it right here with you, because you are really forgiving *yourself* for being caught up in the dream too. They know not what they do, nor to whom they do it; but *you* do. Now. At last. Take hope! One aspect of Your Self has already made it, and paved the way for you: Jesus. This is why He said, "Love your neighbor as yourself," because your neighbor literally IS yourself! This is why treating others with kindness is so important. You can only help *yourself* through your own kindness and compassion. This is why Jesus was able to truly love His enemies. He knew they were just aspects of Himself that were living in the darkness of the illusion. The purpose of His crucifixion was to demonstrate the way Home through extending only His Love and forgiveness in response to all suffering. He was the ultimate example of how to use forgiveness. He never got caught up in the illusion. He is within each of you, and it is *Him* you must see in everyone. It is Christ's face you look upon when you see your brothers. Therefore, never make things harder for another, or create drama that draws them deeper into the illusion. You are only hurting yourself in another life. However, you cannot see both the body and Christ within them at the same time. You have to *choose* how you'd like to see everyone. So, give yourself a break! See others gently, and know you/they are doing the best you/they can, with what you've all chosen to take on. You cannot judge them, because you don't remember what you/they had to go through in that lifetime which lead to the choices you/they made. Forgive them. They are you, and you see them not as they really are.

ME: Okay. This is a lot to think about, but I'll try to take it in. I think I can process this. Thank You for helping me understand this so clearly. But I have one last question. Why didn't you speak to me while I was safe in bed meditating this morning? I mean, I was riding my motorcycle when You revealed this to me. With a revelation as shocking as this, I could've run off the road!

HS: I tried to speak to you this morning, but your rambling ego mind wouldn't be quiet long enough for you to hear Me. You see, I will never force Myself on anyone. *You* have to come to *Me*. In quietness are all things answered. You have to be in the correct state of mind to be able to hear Me. It wasn't until you were riding your motorcycle, lost in the sunrise and smells of spring, that your ego mind quit thinking long enough for you to hear Me.

ME: Huh. I thought I *was* quiet during mediation this morning.

HS: Therein lies your problem. You *thought*. Thinking is what gets you into trouble.

ME: Ah. Gotcha. I think.

HS: No, don't think.

ME: Good grief! Right.

HS: Now, just to clarify, you are all here for the same purpose; to forgive this reality and return Home. Everyone here has an important job to do. Everyone here has taken on a piece of the world to forgive. You've each taken on different lifetimes for each other with different scenarios to experience, with seemingly different lessons in forgiveness. Yet, they are all the same. Your only business is forgiveness.

ME: But some people's lives appear absolutely dreadful! That hardly seems fair.

HS: Quote please.

The following quotations from the Course are from TEXT Chapter 25 — VI. The Special Function

"Forgiveness is the only function meaningful in time. It is the means the Holy Spirit uses to translate specialness from sin into salvation. Forgiveness is for all. But when it rests on all it is complete, and every function of this world completed within. Then is time no more. Yet while in time, there is still much to do. And each must do what is allotted him, for on his part does all the plan depend. He *has* a special part in time for so he chose, and choosing it, he made it for himself. His wish was not denied but changed in form, to let it serve his brother and himself, and thus become a means to save instead of lose." (5:3-9)

"Salvation is no more than a reminder this world is not your home. It's laws are not imposed on you, it's values are not yours. And nothing that you think you see in it is really there at all." (6:1-3)

"The Holy Spirit needs your special function, that His may be fulfilled. Think not you lack a special value here." (7:1-2)

"Only in darkness does your specialness appear to be attack. In light, you see it as your special function in the plan to save the Son of God from all attack, and let him understand that he is safe, as he had always been, and will remain in time and in eternity alike." (7:6-10)

HS: All forgiveness lessons are perfectly "fair" because you have each chosen your own special lessons. This should inspire deep gratitude within you. Look with deepest appreciation upon your fellow brothers for the hardships they've chosen in order that your Self may return Home. Judgment is unwarranted. Be grateful to each and every person for bearing his or her part.

ME: Oh! That's why no one can awaken alone. This is why we truly need each other. This is why what we *give* we also *receive*. Forgiveness then, is the means for our mutual release from what we see. We are One. What I give to another, I am giving to myself.

HS: Yes. Therefore, act accordingly. Extend only mercy and forgiveness to those you see or think of. They agreed to come here to help you on your path to salvation. They each have a part to play. Some have agreed to play the "bad guy" and challenge you in your greatest lessons in forgiveness, while others are here only for your love and support.

ME: Sometimes I think it's hard to tell the difference.

HS: It doesn't matter. Don't judge their chosen role either way. You all truly love one another, but have only forgotten it. You *all* agreed to the script before you came here. Thank your friends, thank your enemies. None of you can do it without the other. Once you are all aware of Who You Are, you will greet each other with loving gratitude for all that you've done for one another. One day you will each awaken to One Love, and in that holy instant will salvation come.

Chapter 18: Lessons 241-250

We Live A Virtual Existence

241. This holy instant is salvation come.

HS: The holy instant is the moment you decide to extend complete and total forgiveness. It is the moment you no longer feel fear in any form. The holy instant is the realization that none of this is true, and you are only Love. You are then saved from what you once believed. This realization releases the world from your ego's perception and adjusts it to the seeing eyes of the Holy Spirit. You can make the choice for the holy instant today. Give this day to God. Let it be your gift to Him.

242. This day is God's. It is my gift to Him.

HS: All life is sustained and united by God. Yet, you do not recognize Him in it, because you see all Life living as separated parts. Your vision of Unity and Oneness was seemingly shattered when you thought you could dream a dream of separation. Yet God is all around you, awaiting your permission to show you His Reassembled Self. You have shattered nothing. You must forgive what you see, which grants Him your permission to show you the Unity He Created. He will not forcefully take this world from your grasp. He will not demand that you give up all His pieces immediately. You must choose to gently lay each one down at His feet, undesired, with a heart full of forgiveness; judging nothing that occurs in this world.

243. Today I will judge nothing that occurs.

HS: You are not fit to judge anything, because you see the world through eyes designed to see only illusion and dreams. The eyes of the body will not show you truth. This is why the world is so confusing. Your eyes and ears tell you only lies, but your heart knows the truth. And so, you are confused and deceived. You cannot see what lies beyond the world of form; you cannot see the eternal Love and Constancy that abides in the complete Safety that is God. Give honor to each brother, knowing he contains God, though you cannot see Him through his bodily form; and that you are in danger nowhere in the world.

244. I am in danger nowhere in the world.

HS: How can this be true? There appears to be danger all around you. The ego believes it is alone and unsafe in the world, yet you are completely unaware that God surrounds you completely. You cannot understand or know this, given the state of your mind as it is now. You can only take it on faith that you are beloved of your Father. The ego imagines exactly the opposite; that you suffer, live in a world of constant fear, and then you die. Instead, remember always that His peace is with you, and you are safe.

245. Your peace is with me, Father. I am safe.

HS: In reality, you exist in total peace and safety. There is nothing to fear when there is only One. There is no conflict, no split, no division into "otherness." Only peace. Only stillness. You are bonded together by God your Father, and so to love your Father is to love His Son.

246. To love my Father is to love His Son.

HS: To love your Father, you *must* also love His Son, for you are each a member of His Sonship. Yet, you mistakenly see His Son in a separate body. This mistake causes you to have feelings of hate, resentment, fear and anxiety towards Him instead of love. You do not know Whom it is you despise. Through forgiveness, you must accept that He is not a body and love Him in whatever form He may appear to you. For without forgiveness you will still be blind.

247. Without forgiveness I will still be blind.

HS: Forgiveness allows you to see past all errors within this illusion. Forgiveness undoes sin. Sin is nothing more than an error in sight, arising from a lack of love. Forgiveness will not cause people to look any differently to you on the outside, but it will cause you to feel differently towards them *on the inside*. You will no longer be blind when this inner shift occurs, and all your suffering will cease. When you feel suffering, you are feeling an un-forgiveness, and whatever suffers is not part of you.

248. Whatever suffers is not part of me.

HS: You have worked hard to forget your Perfect Union. So much so, that you no longer believe in it. You believe in your pain and suffering instead. This is insanity. The entire world of separation you see, is backwards. The only way to undo this backward perception is to forgive it. Forgive every form of suffering within, for forgiveness ends all suffering and loss.

249. Forgiveness ends all suffering and loss.

HS: What causes you to suffer so? What is it you have lost? You suffer only from the thought that you have somehow separated from God. Yet, this is not true. It is only the *memory* of your Union in Him that you have lost, and it is this error in thought that lies at the bottom of every problem you suffer from. You all suffer from the same "separation anxiety." This is the only thought you need to heal in order to find salvation. And so your long journey away from Home will end, as your mind is returned to His Light, Love, and total Union. You will no longer see yourself as limited to a body.

250. Let me not see myself as limited.

HS: The body is a limitation you have placed upon yourself. It obscures your Light, just as clouds obscure the sun. Yet, just as you know the sun is always behind the clouds, know that God's Son is always behind the body. Do not judge what you see outside yourself, but remember instead that you are perfect within. The body hides your perfection. Without the body, you are all equal. You are all equally perfect in God's Love and Light. This is hard to imagine while within the illusion, yet this imagining is your inner vision and it will show you truth.

. . .

ME: You know, these lessons about seeing with our inner vision instead of believing what our eyes show us, reminds me of a dream I had about reality being all one big simulation.

HS: Yes. That dream was an accurate portrayal of how things are for you in the illusion while you dream you are in a body.

ME: Can we talk about dreams for just a second? What are they? Sometimes I have pleasant ones, sometimes nightmares, and some don't seem to make any sense at all. And since I began studying the Course, I've occasionally noticed dreams that are highly vivid and spiritually symbolic.

HS: Dreams have several purposes. Know that few are significant, and are merely the ego expressing itself; they are just as meaningless as your waking illusionary life. However, some *do* have special meaning and are truly messages sent to you as helpful aid, such as the ones you recognize as being spiritually significant. There will always be one tell tale sign as to when a dream is a spiritual message from Me or just your ego expressing itself; My dreams will always end with love. Nightmares on the other hand, are the deep fears of the ego being released. Still, take some comfort in having them; they are also a sign of progress. It is better to have your fears expressed through sleeping nightmares, rather than to be made manifest as illness in the body. Fear makes you sick. It must be dissipated one way or another. It can be released through dreaming a nightmare, experiencing a waking nightmare of pain and sickness, or dispelled entirely through forgiveness. In time, as you become better at forgiving, you will notice a shift in your sleeping dreams from ones of fear, to ones of peace. Through your forgivenesses, first your sleeping dreams will turn happy, and then your waking dreams will become happy.

The following quotations from the Course are from TEXT Chapter 13 — VII. Attainment of the Real World

"You will first dream of peace, and then awaken to it. Your first exchange of what you made for what you want is the change of nightmares for the happy dreams of love." (9:1-2)

"Love waits on welcome, not on time, and the real world is but your welcome of what always was." (9:7)

"Whenever you are tempted to undertake a useless journey that would lead away from light, remember what you really want, and say: *The Holy Spirit leads me unto Christ, and where else would I go? What need have I but to awake in Him?*" (14:1-3)

"Then follow Him in joy, with faith that He will lead you safely through all dangers to your peace of mind this world may set before you." (15:1)

HS: And so, I will use every aspect of your experience in this illusion to awaken you. I will use both sleeping dreams and what you deem reality to your advantage. No dream, no experience, and no relationship is ever wasted. All are carefully coordinated; directing you towards your speedy awakening.

The following quotations from the Course are from TEXT Chapter 18 — II. The Basis of the Dream

"The Holy Spirit, ever practical in His wisdom, accepts your dreams and uses them as means for waking. You would have used them to remain asleep. I said before that the first change, before dreams disappear, is that your dreams of fear are changed to happy dreams." (6:1-3)

"Let not the dream take hold to close your eyes. It is not strange that dreams can make a world that is unreal. It is the *wish* to make it that is incredible." (8:1-3)

"Yet Heaven is sure. This is no dream. Its coming means that you have chosen truth, and it has come because you have been willing to let your special relationships meet its conditions." (9:1-3)

ME: Yes, I've certainly noticed a shift in my dreams since I began studying the Course. Not too long ago, I had a dream about this world being all just one big simulation; that nothing my eyes saw was real, but rather, just a projection from a pair of goggles I was wearing. The dream started out terrifying; I was flying above some mountains in a chair without any harness or seatbelt. It was soaring through the air all topsy turvy in every direction, and yet, to my disbelief, I wasn't falling out. Then I realized my toes were still touching the hard surface of the ground; I just couldn't see that they were doing so.

Once the "ride" ended, I took off the goggles only to see that I had been safe on the ground the whole time. None of it had been real. I hadn't actually gone anywhere at all. I'd been completely safe the whole time, despite my fear of dying.

HS: You may feel as though everything around you is completely real, but it is not. It may appear that you can be hurt both physically and emotionally, but your real Self is safe at Home, in God's loving Arms; where your soul remains intact and protected from all harm, safe in Heaven. Indeed, you have placed goggles over your eyes that project a different world than what is truth.

ME: So life still has the same effect, but it's even better if we know we can't be harmed.

HS: Yes. Love Life! Enjoy it to the fullest. No true harm can come you, no matter how fearful the ride.

ME: So we're actually being blessed by the fact nothing we see is real?

HS: Correct. Everyone takes life too seriously. Nothing is ever truly a "life and death" situation, because nobody can die. You are all forever only Life. So "lighten up" and enjoy the ride. Know you are safe, despite the fearful world you see around you. This is the truth and the truth is all you need.

Chapter 19: Lessons 251-260

My Past Life During The Time of Jesus

251. I am in need of nothing but the truth.

HS: The truth is, you are God's Holy Child, One in His Sonship, which He created as One with Himself. Nothing else exists. Only this is real. Knowing this truth is all you need to heal yourself and the world. Accepting this truth will undo all separation that you see around you. There is nothing else you need, but to accept the truth of your Identity as God's holy Son.

252. The Son of God is my Identity.

HS: It seems impossible to have to forgotten Who You Are. Yet, I ask that you awaken to your true Identity. You hold the power of God within it. It is God's Will that you remember your Self, Who is ruler of the universe.

253. My Self is ruler of the universe.

HS: There are no coincidences in the universe. Everything you see, everything you experience, you have *asked for* through the tenor of your thoughts. Your Self, that still abides with God and remembers Him, is fully aware of this. Your Self sends you everything you need to awaken from this dream. Nothing does or doesn't happen without the approval of your Self. You are not at the mercy of any devil or god, helpless and victimized, and neither are you at the mercy of chance. You are doing everything to yourself. Your Self is ruler of the universe, but you have chosen to block this Voice out, and allow your ego to rule in its place. How merciful has your ego been to you? Let every voice but God's be still in you.

254. Let every voice but God's be still in me.

HS: The ego will do its best to obscure the Voice of God within you with all its problems, anxieties, pain, and stress. Quietly step back from all this and see these thoughts for what they are; false images of separation. Then let them all go. You do not want anxiety, you want peace. In silence, choose to spend your time in perfect peace.

255. This day I choose to spend in perfect peace.

HS: Attaining perfect peace may seem like an impossible achievement. This world pulls your thoughts in a million different directions, in a million different ways. Some thoughts are of past events you are re-playing, while others are fears about a future you cannot know. Either way, it all creates restlessness and anxiety. You must let go of every fear through forgiving them; keep no thoughts that are not peaceful. Peace has to be *chosen*. The minute you let your guard down, the ego will gladly step in and raise negative mayhem within your mind. Make God the only goal you have.

256. God is the only goal I have today.

HS: You will be content only through achieving the one goal you came here to achieve: remembering your Oneness in God. You have no other goal but this. You have no other purpose but this. Do not forget what your purpose here is.

257. Let me remember what my purpose is.

HS: Remember you are not in conflict with anyone, despite what circumstances may show you. You cannot be in conflict, because in truth, you are One. Something that is truly whole, is not broken into conflicting parts. Underneath all the fuss, the drama, and the confusion, lies your Wholeness in Me. Remember that your goal is God.

258. Let me remember that my goal is God.

HS: You are living under false pretenses. You think your goals are of this world. This causes you endless misery and striving. This world will never be enough. All you need to do to escape this insane cycle, is to change your mind about what your goal is. All these meaningless, endless distractions cover the real truth; you want peace. Nothing in the world will bring you this. Live in the world, enjoy it, but do not want it more than Me. You see only a world of sin and error all around you. It is not real. Remember that there is no sin.

259. Let me remember that there is no sin.

HS: Have you never wondered why you cannot take anything from this world with you when your body dies? It is because none of it is eternal, and therefore none of it is real. Only what is eternal can transfer into God's Kingdom. God doesn't want anything you've made with your ego. It is all sin. Sin is anything lacking eternal qualities, and something that is not eternal, cannot be brought into an eternal reality. Remember, *God* created you.

260. Let me remember God created me.

HS: From the time you are born, you are taught you are a body by others who are equally convinced that they are are bodies. None of you can remember your true Identity. You cannot see the Life Force that unites you all. You cannot see your Source. You are living in this world, blind as bats. Yet even bats have found another way to see without using their eyes. As can you. You must learn to see that you are One, equal and united by your holy Source. Have mercy upon yourself and look lovingly upon one another.

. . .

ME: I want to remember everything about You and Heaven. I really do. I just don't feel like I'm making any progress. It's as though I try and I try, yet my mind seems to stay the same as it always was.

HS: You may not see much in the way of outward progress at times, but I promise you, your forgiveness efforts *are* having an effect in the world of Spirit; the *real* world. And the effects of your forgivenesses in the present moment, directly affect your experience here in the illusion; both past and future. But you must make the choice to forgive *now* in order to change your experience here.

ME: You know, I have a past life memory of when I made a choice in the present moment like You're describing. It was by far one of the most startling things You've ever revealed to me.

HS: That past life was when you first heard the message of *A Course in Miracles*. It was My First Coming. My Second Coming will be when you decide to return to Me; this can also be called your resurrection, or the Atonement. Through your acceptance of your Sonship in Me, I will come again through your heart. And so the illusion will come to an end for you. This will happen to every human being in time. How far off that time may be, is up to each individual.

ME: So it's the choice to seek to know only my Unity with You, and this choice causes me to be freed from the illusion?

HS: Correct.

ME: I feel I should briefly share what happened to me during that past life, when I met You here in the illusion as the man Jesus.

HS: Please do that.

ME: I was an ill tempered, mean fisherman named Silian, and was married with four children. We lived along the Sea of Galilee, not far from Tiberias. I had no loving thoughts towards anyone, and could call no one my friend. Then one day, I heard Jesus would be speaking nearby where we lived. I wanted to attend this event; not to hear what He had to say, but rather see what He looked like. People said He was the Son of God. I wanted to see for myself if He indeed *looked* like the Son of God.

When I reached Him, instead of having an outer experience of judging His appearance, I had an inner transformation of loving Him. I had made only the briefest of eye contact with Him, but in those few seconds, something unexplainable came to life within me; something sublimely good and pure. I was deeply compelled by a Great Love and Goodness to be more than what I thought I was.

This event forever changed me. From that point on, I worked hard to choose love in every moment. My temper, my lack of love for others, and my intolerance, all dissolved as I put forth my best willingness to be what Jesus had seen in me. *Now* I was working towards my final destiny. *Now* my living had truly begun.

HS: You, and many others on the planet now, were with Me when I was came into the illusion as the man Jesus. This is your second chance to study My message of truth; presented to you in a form so complete and undeniably clear that you can't miss it unless you refuse to see it.

ME: So apparently I hadn't completely gotten it that first time around when You taught it 2000 years ago while here on earth, and now I am here to complete my learning? Is that why when I held the Course in my hands at the bookstore over a decade ago, I clearly heard the words, "Read this. Do not miss this message for the second time around. You will be unhappy with yourself if you do." Was that what You were talking about? This is a second chance for me to learn Your message?

HS: Yes, you are here to learn to love everyone, as Christ has loved you. This is what you are *all* here to do. Through your love and forgiveness, you can transcend this reality and return Home. And no one goes alone. You need each other to accomplish this, because You are One Love. You are One in this purpose, and not one of you will be left behind.

ME: So there were many other people who were healed by Jesus like I was? I suppose that's true- He spoke to thousands on multiple occasions.

HS: Yes, many of you who were with Christ then, are here now to fulfill your promise to Him to love one another as He loves you. By following His Way, you bring Heaven to earth through your loving thoughts; The Second Coming of Christ. Knowing this, take your refuge and security in only Him, who is within each of you.

Chapter 20: Lessons 261-270

True Gratitude

261. God is my refuge and security.

HS: You will never find refuge or security within the body. It is an idol you have made, that you worshipfully maintain with your last dying effort. Yet, all to no avail. Every body dies. Gratefully, it is not who you are. Forgive it and understand you live in God. Honorably take care of the body for as long as you dream you are in it, but never lose sight of the fact that the body is not a worthy identity for you. Your true Identity holds no differences between you.

262. Let me perceive no differences today.

HS: There can be no conflict, where there is no difference. All the various of forms you see, show differences between each of you. The body's vision rests strictly on surface appearances only. Within, you are all part of God's One Sonship. Do not see a stranger. Christ is here. Among you now. There is peace in recognition of Him, because there can be no differences or conflict where there is Perfect Unity. Your holy vision sees all things as pure and whole.

263. My holy vision sees all things as pure.

HS: You live, move, and breathe in God. All living things are part of His Life. You cannot see His Life with your bodily eyes, but you can trust it is there. You know this to be true, because you exist. All living things are imbued with the Life of God, and so all living things are pure. Through your holy vision, you will see all living things surrounded by the Love of God.

264. I am surrounded by the Love of God.

HS: There is nowhere that God is not. You can read these words, and agree with them, but it is difficult to remember in everyday circumstances. You are surrounded by the Love of God. This is what you want to experience; the Love of God surrounding you. This experience is salvation from the world. It is the Holy Instant. The world is saved when you forgive it, by choosing to remember Creation's gentleness in all you see.

144

265. Creation's gentleness is all I see.

HS: This may seem impossible. How do you see gentleness, when conflict is all around you? You must learn to use your inner vision. You cannot see God with your bodily eyes, but you can see Him with your inner eyes. You can change what you see, through changing your thoughts. The secret to salvation is only this; to realize that you are doing this to yourself. Use your inner sight to see your holy Self abiding within God's Son instead.

266. My holy Self abides in you, God's Son.

HS: You are each other's saviors. No one can be saved from this illusion alone. The way to salvation, is to acknowledge the Light within one another. This Unifying Light abides in every person you see. If you see your holy Self within even *one* of them, you will see your Self in *all*. You will be saved at last. How can you lose your way, when so many surround you, waiting to bring you to salvation? Know that each of your hearts beat in the peace of God.

267. My heart is beating in the peace of God.

HS: The only time your physical heart ever rests, is between each beat. God is the peace between each heartbeat. You can feel God's holy Presence within you, beating your heart, and breathing your lungs. In this way, the body can become holy in your vision, as it is seen as imbued with the Life and Breath of God; as you truly are. Let all things be exactly as they are.

268. Let all things be exactly as they are.

HS: What do things look like, when they are allowed to be *exactly as they are*? They look like Love. They look like peace. It is a state of being that is entirely without conflict, comparison, or judgement. Because you have imposed your judgement upon all you see, deciding in advance that you know what the truth is, the truth is obscured. Love is what lies behind all types of form. See the world and everyone in it, as they were created by God; not as they appear to you now. Allow your sight to go forth to look upon Christ's face.

269. My sight goes forth to look upon Christ's face.

HS: It is difficult to see anything beyond what your eyes behold. Therefore, you need assistance in seeing the world through the filter of My eyes. Attain

My holy Vision through the willingness to forgive the world as it is now, and look beyond it, to the world that transcends this one. There will you find Unity. There will you find equal eternal love for all. You will see how you are all connected by One Love. Decide not use the body's eyes to see.

270. I will not use the body's eyes today.

HS: Through your forgiveness of everything you see in the world, you signify to God that you are ready to see all things as they truly are. You signify to Him that you are ready to have your entire memory restored. Your thoughts must become so forgiving that they contain no conflict, no judgment, and no condemnation. Your thoughts must be still, and see the world forgiven.

. . .

ME: Ah, the forgiven world. Sometimes I feel as though I'm at peace with the world; that I've forgiven it, and everyone in it; then a second later something happens and I'm not at peace anymore. I wish it would last. It's as though I'm being purposely sabotaged by outside forces, determined to ruin it for me. I just can't seem to change the way I see people. Everyone remains just as aggravating as always, no matter how hard I try to see them differently.

HS: Therein lies your problem. You think the world and everyone in it is against you, when in fact, it is only *you* against *yourself*. You are missing a key element to your thinking. You are not seeing them through the eyes of gratitude. I would like you to go back and take a second look at lesson 197 again. You are forgetting what true gratitude is. Please share that lesson here now, quoting specific sentences as I instruct.

Lesson 197

It can be but my gratitude I earn.

"Here is the second step we take to free your mind from the belief in outside force pitted against your own. You make attempts at kindness and forgiveness. Yet you turn them to attack again, unless you find external gratitude and lavish thanks. (1:1-3)

146

It does not matter if another thinks your gifts unworthy. In his mind there is a part that joins with yours in thanking you. (4:1-2)

God blesses every gift you give to Him, and every gift is given Him, because it can be given only to yourself. (5:1)

Thanks be to you, the holy Son of God. For as you were created, you contain all things within your Self. And you are still as God created you. (8:1-3)

Be you free of all ingratitude to anyone who makes your Self complete. (9:2)

Give thanks for all the countless channels which extend this Self." (9:4)

ME: So I should be grateful for everyone around me, because they are all channels extending from my one Self? Got it. I will try to manage to see all people that way. Even the irritating ones.

HS: Yes, but there is more to it than that.

ME: Sigh. Of course there is. Funny, I am reminded of another dream. I had it a couple of years ago, on the very night after I finished reading the entire *Course* for the first time. I wrote it down because it seemed so real and spiritually significant.

HS: It would be appropriate for you to briefly share that here now.

ME: Oh, alright. Except I don't see what it has to do with gratitude.

On Sunday, October 12th, 2014 I had just completed reading *A Course in Miracles* for the first time. That night, I had a very strange and vivid dream. A dream that I can only describe as feeling like some sort of test. In hindsight, I suppose it's only fitting that my completion of the Course be followed by some type of "final exam."

I dreamt that I had found a bag full of money. Upon inspecting the bag, I realized the money belonged to a restaurant owner that I knew. When

I went to return the money to her, instead of reacting with joy and gratitude as I had expected, she seemed agitated and almost annoyed that I had bothered her about it.

HS: And what was your reaction to her response?

ME: Well, I was shocked at first. Her reaction was not what I had expected. Then, at that point in the dream, I heard a Voice ask me, "Does it bother you that she is ungrateful?"

After thinking about this for a second, I stood up straight and replied, "No. I didn't return the money to earn her gratitude. I returned it, because it was the right thing to do."

HS: And My reply to you was, "Very good. You pass."

ME: So the test in the dream was about gratitude? I always thought this dream was about whether or not I should return the money.

HS: That you should've returned the money is obvious. It was never about that. The important question, was whether or not you truly understood gratitude.

ME: Well I'm glad I passed, but I think I need further explanation here. Apparently I only understood it in my sleep.

HS: Divine gratitude is not about being grateful for having more or less, or being better or worse than anyone else. It is not about *differences* between yourself and others. Divine gratitude is to be grateful for your *sameness*. True gratitude has nothing to do with the body or the world. True gratitude is to be grateful for only one thing: You have never truly separated from one another. It is to be grateful you each contain the same Loving Spirit; your one Self in God. Nothing more, nothing less. Likewise, you should never expect gratitude in return from anyone. Nobody owes you gratitude for anything, because there is nothing to owe you in your Oneness. Again, true gratitude has nothing to do with the world and what you've done for someone else. You don't need to *do* anything to *earn* gratitude, because you already *have* it. You are one Self. All forms of gratitude that stem from this world are not divine. Be grateful only that you and your fellows each equally carry My Light and Love.

ME: So *that's* what the test was about? Whether or not I'd be upset by the woman's lack of gratitude?

HS: Correct. And you passed perfectly. You didn't mind not having her gratitude, because you recognized it was not the motive behind your actions. Being kind, helpful, and honest were your true motives; the motives of Spirit. Had you taken offense to her reaction, you would have demonstrated the ego's view of gratitude, which is that she owed you her gratitude for returning her money. In truth, she owes you nothing because you lack nothing. You are whole and complete unto your One Self. If you would've looked at her through the eyes of the ego, you would've taken offense to her reaction and thrown away your happiness and peace.

ME: I think I get it. This is part of learning to look past the body everyone appears to be in, right? If I don't believe they are a body, then I shouldn't be offended by anything they do with it. I need to remind myself it isn't who they truly are, and be grateful we are One in truth.

HS: Correct.

ME: But what about the things in this world I truly feel grateful for? Like my family, health, home, sunrises and all that? Isn't it appropriate that I be grateful for those things?

HS: Even those things are temptations to believe this world is real. You may enjoy them, but do not think they are what brings you happiness. As soon as they are gone, you will feel sorrow. The joy these things bring is not eternal. There is only one Source from which all joy and gratitude flows eternally. All else is of this world and will eventually cause you to suffer through its seeming loss. Though it is not wrong to enjoy these things, be careful to forgive it all equally, knowing it is still a from of separation. There is a quote I'd like you to put here.

**The following quotations from the Course are from
TEXT Chapter 26 — VI. The Appointed Friend**

> "Anything in this world that you believe is good and valuable and worth striving for can hurt you, and will do so. Not because it has the power to hurt, but just because you have denied it is but an illusion, and made it real." (1:1-2)

> "Make no illusion friend, for if you do, it can but take the place of Him Whom God has Called your Friend. And it is He Who is your only Friend in truth. He brings you gifts that are not of this world, and only He to Whom they have been given can make sure that you receive them. He will place them on your throne, when you make room for Him on His." (3:3-6)

ME: Okay. Well now I feel guilty for enjoying anything at all in this world. You make it sound like I'm putting everything fun ahead of You. I'm not seriously trying to do that. I just happen to enjoy some parts of this illusion more than others, and I am grateful for them. And You're... Well... I can't even *see* You, so these things kind of move in front of You sometimes. By accident.

HS: Just understand that all the love and gratitude you may feel towards this world, is really for My Love that lies behind it. Keep in mind that you are actually grateful for the Oneness that lies behind the illusion, rather than for the illusion itself. Seeing the world this way is the beginning of the attainment of Christ's vision.

Chapter 21: Lessons 271-280

The Justice of God

271. Christ's is the vision I will use today.

HS: What you think you are, is what you will experience. See only the Christ within one another and you invite the memory of God to be restored to you. Heaven will become the reality you see, instead of this illusion. Know that the illusions of this world will never satisfy you.

272. How can illusions satisfy God's Son?

HS: No one has ever been satisfied with what is not real. As children, you played imaginary games. These games were never wholly satisfying, because you knew they weren't real. Yet, you kept playing them until you grew tired of them. This world is your playground and as long as there is something here you think you want more than My peace, you will continue to return. You will know whenever you forget what you want, by your feeling of discontent. When this happens, simply remember to ask yourself: Can an illusion satisfy God's Son? No. Choose the stillness and peace of God instead of this world.

273. The stillness of the peace of God is mine.

HS: The stillness of the peace of God is yours. This is your natural state of being. By claiming your peace now, you ensure that it will extend on into the future. This moment belongs to love. You have nothing to fear.

274. Today belongs to love. Let me not fear.

HS: Love is the true state of all living things. Love is what you are. Honor another's True Identity, by bestowing upon them the love and kindness that is their due, no matter how loveless the form you may see. Your Friend is within them, though you cannot see Him or hear His Voice. God's healing Voice protects all things.

275. God's healing Voice protects all things today.

HS: You need not worry about, nor fear anything. Trust yourself to My

Voice. I will instruct you in all things, and so leave all things to Me. I will guide you lovingly and without error. My Word is given you to speak to all whom I send to you.

276. The Word of God is given me to speak.

HS: God's Word, is a *living Word.* In order to make My Word yours, you must *live* It. Everyone is here for you to love. My Word, is that you love your brothers as I love them; without conditions, expectations, or regard to their form. You are not bound to the false laws of fear and separation here within the illusion. Do not bind God's Son with laws you made.

277. Let me not bind Your Son with laws I made.

HS: You are God's holy Son. You remain unchanged by your wild imaginings. God holds the memory of your perfection for you. The memory of the truth of Who You Are, will be returned to you once you cease to bind God's Son within the laws of the body. When you believe yourself to be a body, you are bound, and God is not free to give you the memory you're entitled to. By deciding you're a body, you're saying you don't want to remember your Self. God will not deny you what you want. If you want to be bound, your Father is not free.

278. If I am bound, my Father is not free.

HS: You cannot have two identities. You either bind yourself to a body, or are free in God's Sonship. You want the truth to be your experience. Let go of the dream of fear and separation, and choose to free the world by knowing yourself as Love. Through freeing all God's creation, you are promised your own.

279. Creation's freedom promises my own.

HS: As you look around, you see anything *but* freedom and perfect peace. You wonder, "Where is God in all this suffering?" He has not abandoned you. He has promised you freedom and salvation from all suffering. In fact, you are already released. The door to your prison cell is wide open, the shackles unlocked. God promises you freedom this holy instant. Accept your freedom through forgiveness of the world. God keeps His promises, and withholds nothing from you. It is you who refuse to accept what He offers as long as you desire to be something else, something limited. What limits can you place upon God's Son?

280. What limits can I lay upon God's Son?

HS: You do not have the power to change the Love God Created you as. All you can do is *imagine* you have changed. You can imagine you live in a body as an illusion, but you cannot truly change Who You Are. To undo the illusion, you must relearn to know yourself as Love through extending your love to one another. This is your function in forgiveness.

. . .

ME: I think I understand what forgiveness is on an individual level. I feel like I know what I'm supposed to do personally. However, what are we supposed to do about other people? You know, criminals? I mean, do You intend for us to just let them roam around free, forgiving them of all wrongdoing? They would obviously take full advantage of that, and continue on committing crimes. How should we administer justice, while simultaneously forgiving them?

HS: My definition of justice is quite different from the world's. I will try to explain this within the context of your question.

ME: You've already begun to answer my question somewhat. I say this, because I coincidentally came upon the Course TEXT dealing with justice a few days ago, just after I thought of this question.

HS: There is no such thing as coincidence.

The following quotations from the Course are from TEXT Chapter 25 — VIII. Justice Returned to Love

"There is a kind of justice in salvation of which the world knows nothing. To the world, justice and vengeance are the same, for sinners see justice only as their punishment, perhaps sustained by someone else, but not escaped. The laws of sin demand a victim." (3:1-3)

"You who know not of justice still can ask, and learn the answer. Justice looks on all in the same way. It is not just that one should lack for what another has. For that is vengeance in whatever form it takes." (4:1-4)

"But justice does He know, and knows it well. For He is wholly fair to everyone." (5:3-4)

"To be just is to be fair, and not be vengeful. Fairness and vengeance are impossible, for each one contradicts the other and denies that it is real. It is impossible for you to share the Holy Spirits's justice with a mind that can conceive of specialness at all. Yet how could He be just if He condemns a sinner for the crimes he did not do, but thinks he did? And where would justice be if He demanded of the ones obsessed with the idea of punishment that they lay it aside, unaided, and perceive it is not true?" (5:6-10)

"It is extremely hard for those who still believe sin meaningful to understand the Holy Spirit's justice. They must believe He shares their own confusion, and cannot avoid the vengeance that their own belief in justice must entail." (6:1-2)

"They *do* believe that Heaven is hell, and *are* afraid of love. And deep suspicion and the chill of fear comes over them when they are told that they have never sinned." (6:5-6)

"Yet justice cannot punish those who ask for punishment, but have a Judge Who knows that they are wholly innocent in truth." (8:1)

"For love and justice are not different. *Because* they are the same does mercy stand at God's right Hand, and gives the Son of God the power to forgive himself of sin." (9:10-11)

"God knows of no injustice. He would not allow His Son be judged by those who seek his death, and could not see his worth at all." (10:3-4)

"No justice would be given him by you." (10:7)

"You can be perfect witness to the power of love and justice, if you understand it is impossible the Son of God could merit vengeance. You need not perceive, in every circumstance, that this is true. Nor need you look to your experience within the world, which is but shadows of all that is really happening within yourself. The understanding that you need comes not of you, but from a larger Self, so great and holy that He could not doubt His innocence. Your special function is a call to Him, that He may smile on you whose sinlessness He shares. His understanding will be yours." (12:1-6)

"Judge not because you cannot, not because you are a miserable sinner too." (13:3-4)

"You have the right to all the universe; to perfect peace, complete deliverance from all effects of sin, and to the life eternal, joyous and complete in every way, as God appointed for His holy Son." (14:1)

"And you are safe from vengeance in all forms." (14:4)

"Let love decide, and never fear that you, in your unfairness, will deprive yourself of what God's justice has allotted you." (14:7)

ME: Um. I need You to explain all this to me.

HS: Certainly. I will begin by bringing some ideas together for you. Do you see any difference between My definition of forgiveness, gratitude and justice? There is none. They are each the same. They are each a way of seeing each other as One, rather than separate. You are each equally innocent, whole, and beloved of Me. This being true, how would it be fair for Me to punish some of you for perceived wrongdoing in the illusion, and not others? I am completely just and fair. I extend My Love to you all equally. And so you are safe from vengeance, as I will never treat you unfairly. However, within this world you see things differently. You see each other as separate, unequal, and capable of mistreating one another. God in His justice sees this, and knows you desire order, even in a world of chaos.

ME: So, does this mean You do not believe in worldly punishment in any form?

HS: Remember you are incapable of judging anyone from the point of view you currently hold. You would judge someone as guilty, while you yourself stand next to him in equal guilt. In truth, neither of you is guilty of wrongdoing in this illusion. All are equally innocent. I know this is difficult for you to comprehend while immersed in the dream of separation.

ME: Alright, I understand what You're saying. But what do You suggest we do with criminals while immersed here in the dream of separation?

HS: Those who are so deeply embedded in the illusion, that they think that harming other bodies is the way to achieve happiness, cannot be allowed to wantonly cause fear in those around them without restraint. Under these circumstances, it would be appropriate to contain them if they are unable to do so themselves. The perpetuation of fear in others should always be discouraged and controlled if need be. Increasing fear does not help release people from the illusion of sin, but rather only deepens it.

The following quotations from the Course are from TEXT Chapter 25 — IX. The Justice of Heaven

"Are you willing to be released from all effects of sin? You cannot answer this until you see all that the answer must entail. For if you answer "yes" it means you will forego all values of this world in favor of the peace of Heaven." (1:3-5)

"You mean that truth has greater value now than all illusions. And you recognize that truth must be revealed to you, because you know not what it is." (1:8-9)

"Be certain any answer to a problem the Holy Spirit solves will always be one in which no one loses. And this must be true, because He asks no sacrifice of anyone." (3:1-2)

"The Holy Spirit's problem solving is the way in which the problem ends. It has been solved because it has been met with justice. Until it has it will recur, because it has not yet been solved. The principle that justice means no one can lose is crucial to this course. For miracles depend on justice. Not as it is seen through this world's eyes, but as God knows it and as knowledge is reflected in the sight the Holy Spirit gives." (5:1-6)

"Healing must be for everyone, because he does not merit an attack of any kind. What order can there be in miracles, unless someone deserves to suffer more and others less?" (6:3-4)

"A miracle *is* justice. It is not a special gift to some, to be withheld from others as less worthy, more condemned, and thus apart from healing." (6:6-7)

"The miracle that you receive, you give. Each one becomes an illustration of the law on which salvation rests; that justice must be done to all, if anyone is to be healed." (10:1-2)

"It is awareness that giving and receiving are the same." (10:6)

"Its offering is universal and it teaches but one message: *What is God's belongs to everyone, and is his due.*" (10:9-10)

HS: And so it is true what Jesus said in the bible, "Render therefore unto Caesar the things which are Caesar's: and unto God the things that are God's." (Matthew 22:21). Deal with the unseeing people of this world as you must, so that they do not make the journey to Me more difficult for others. But do so with love and great wisdom; understanding that what you do to them, you do to Me also, and yourself as well. They do not merit attack from you, but rather, your love and forgiveness. See them as they are in truth; equally beloved of God and innocent as your One Self. This way, you avoid hurting yourself through your own thoughts.

Chapter 22: Lessons 281-290

Miracles and Medicine

281. I can be hurt by nothing but my thoughts.

HS: You can be sure, that any time you suffer from sadness, anxiety, pain, or worry, you are hearing the voice of the ego instead of Mine. This is the great secret the ego would never have you discover: that you are hurt only by your own thoughts. Yet your thoughts can be easily changed. Do not be afraid to think you are Love.

282. I will not be afraid of love today.

HS: The fear of love is a problem you don't even know you have. *Who in their right mind, would ever be afraid of love?* The trouble is, you're *not* in your right mind. Truly insane people do not know they're crazy. They believe their irrational actions are justified, and their thoughts are normal. Such as you are now. If you were sane, and did not fear love, you would not be in this body or have forgotten God. The fear of love is at the crux of all your worldly problems and discomforts. Do not fear to know God, for He is but Love, and so are you. Your true Identity abides in Him.

283. My true Identity abides in You.

HS: Your true Identity abides in the Love that God is. Choose to recognize this, by blessing all living things with your love and forgiveness; knowing you are united in His Love. In this way, you consciously elect to change all thoughts that hurt.

284. I can elect to change all thoughts that hurt.

HS: Your problem has been, that you've thought you were at the mercy of this world, but your thinking is backwards. The world is actually at the mercy of *you*. The world is at the mercy of *how you feel and what you think*. Your thoughts dictate your experience, and you have shown no mercy. The painful thoughts you have, are not your real thoughts. Your real thoughts are very holy, and when allowed to shine bright and clear, you will experience a wholly different, holy reality.

Lesson 285. My holiness shines bright and clear today.

HS: Forgiveness stills all thoughts your ego holds about the world. Forgiveness is how you invite your holy thoughts to shine bright and clear. You have no conflict within. Allow the hush of heaven to hold your heart.

286. The hush of Heaven holds my heart today.

HS: The still hush of Heaven, is your natural state of being. This stillness is what it feels like to have forgiven all things. It is a miracle. It is a holy instant of sanity. You need do nothing but be exactly as you are created; still, peaceful, and hushed within. This how you reach God, and God has promised you can do this. He is your goal, your Father. Only Him.

287. You are my goal, my Father. Only You.

HS: The moments of peace and stillness you allow yourself, signify your readiness to have your memories restored to you. When you are willing to allow peace, you are asking that God enter and replace your dreams with true reality. You are saying to God, that He is your only goal. Only Him. You are showing your willingness to let go of everything the world has to offer. This world offers you too little. God offers you eternal peace, happiness, and joy- everything He is. Why would you hold onto a painful world any longer? You need not abandon all things in the physical while you still enjoy and seem to need them. Just release them in your mind by forgetting what has never happened. Forget the past in everyone.

288. Let me forget my brother's past today.

HS: The memories you cling to of the past are the chains that bind you here to the illusion. They can all be released by remembering this: The people you despise most, are the ones God has sent you to forgive. To forgive them, is to see that they are not a body and have done nothing to you. Release them from their past now, in this holy instant. Love them as God loves them. For what God loves, you too must also love because you are One with Him. You have only forgotten that you love them. The past is over. It has touched you not.

289. The past is over. It can touch me not.

HS: You cannot live in two worlds at the same time. You must choose between the past and the present. Why would you choose to live in a past that is full of pain and misery? Its memory only serves to distract you from the real world that awaits your glad acceptance. Forgiveness is the tool to use to make this happy exchange. Then your present happiness will be all you see.

290. My present happiness is all I see.

HS: It may seem an impossible task to remove every bothersome thought of the past from your mind. You will soon discover, it takes constant inner vigilance to keep your thoughts on the present moment. It can appear at first to take a lot of effort, as the same old thoughts pop up over and over again. In the beginning, you will manage forgiveness for only small periods of time- perhaps only for a second or two- before your mind returns to its old habits. But with practice, you will notice with increasing ability when the ego is in command of your thoughts. Forgiveness brings quiet stillness to your mind, and it is here you will find your present happiness.

. . .

ME: Oh I'd really love to be healed of my ego thoughts. It would be so nice to feel quiet, still, and at peace at all times, under every circumstance. It would be nice to be totally free of discomfort, you know?

HS: My dear child, I will explain this to you as many times as you need, until your understanding is reached. You do all this to yourself. It is you who must choose to be healed. Yet, you cannot heal what you do not understand is in need of healing. You cannot solve a problem you do not know you have. Please share the Laws of Healing here now.

The following quotations from the Course are from TEXT Chapter 26 — VII. The Laws of Healing

"This is *A Course in Miracles*. As such, the laws of healing must be understood before the purpose of the course an be accomplished." (1:1-2)

"All sickness comes from separation. When the separation is denied, it goes." (2:1)

"Yet has God given answer to the world of sickness, which applies to all its forms." (4:2)

"God's answer lies where the belief in sin must be, for only there can its effects be utterly undone and without cause." (5:1)

"Illusions are illusions and are false. Your preference gives them no reality." (6:7-8)

"Forgiveness is the only function here, and serves to bring the joy this world denies to every aspect of God's Son where sin was thought to rule. Perhaps you do not see the role forgiveness plays in ending death and all beliefs that rise from mists of guilt. Sins are beliefs that you impose between your brother and yourself. They limit you to time and place, and give a little space to you, another little space to him. This separating off is symbolized, in your perception, by a body which is clearly separate and a thing apart." (8:5-9)

"Forgiveness takes away what stands between your brother and yourself. It is the wish that you be joined with him, and not apart." (9:1-2)

"Salvation, perfect and complete, asks but a little wish that what is true be true; a little willingness to overlook what is not there; a little sigh that speaks for Heaven as a preference to this world that death and desolation seem to rule." (10:1)

"What is the Will of God? He wills His Son have everything. And this He guaranteed when He created him *as* everything." (11:1-3)

"Here does the Son of God ask not too much, but far too little. He would sacrifice his own identity with everything, to find a little treasure of his own. And this he cannot do without a sense of isolation, loss and loneliness." (11:7-9)

"Let us consider what the error is, so it can be corrected, not protected. Sin is belief attack can be projected outside the mind where the belief arose." (12:1-2)

"God wills you learn what always has been true: that He created you as part of Him, and this must still be true because ideas leave not their source. Such is creation's law; that each idea the mind conceives but adds to its abundance, never takes away. This is as true of what is idly wished as what is truly willed, because the mind can wish to be deceived, but cannot make it be what it is not. And to believe ideas can leave their source is to invite illusions to be true, without success. For never will success be possible in trying to deceive the Son of God." (13:2-6)

"Forgiveness is the answer to attack of any kind. So is attack deprived of its effects, and hate is answered in the name of love." (17:2-3)

"To use the power God has given you as He would have it used is natural. It is not arrogant to be as He created you, nor to make use of what He gave to answer all His Son's mistakes and set him free." (18:1-3)

"Abide in peace, where God would have you be. And be the means whereby your brother finds the peace in which your wishes are fulfilled." (19:1-2)

ME: So to heal my mind and body, all I need to do is forgive our separation?

HS: Yes. All you need to heal yourself is to forgive yourself the illusion you are a body. All sickness stems from the idea you are separate from Me and one another. Sickness is a form of conflict. When you are physically sick, your very cells are in conflict. It is only inner peace that can bring everything back into peaceful alignment.

ME: What about taking medicine? Is it wrong to do that? I'm a pharmacist after all, so I'm wondering if I'm perpetuating the illusion and making it harder for people to heal themselves.

HS: As for taking medicine, of course that's fine. You must heal yourself using the means that causes you the least amount of fear, for it is fear that perpetuates sickness. Sick thoughts beget sick bodies. If all medicine were suddenly forbidden, people would be thrown into a panic; not ready to see themselves as healed. Some would literally die of fright. Just know, it isn't the medicine itself that heals the body, but the thought behind it.

ME: So medicine only works because we believe it does?

HS: Yes. If you believe something within the illusion has the power to heal you, then you will be healed. The medicine itself does nothing, because it *is* nothing, just as the body is nothing. However, it is important that you keep using medicine while it still has effects for you. As long as you are afraid to experience the miracle of healing through Me directly, different forms of medicine *must* be used. All healing is simply your release from fear.

The following quotations from the Course are from
TEXT Chapter 2 — IV. Healing as Release from Fear

"The kind of error to which Atonement is applied is irrelevant. All healing is essentially the release from fear. To undertake this you cannot be fearful yourself. You do not understand healing because of your own fear." (1:6-9)

"The body can act wrongly only when it is responding to misthought. The body cannot create, and the belief that it can, a fundamental error, produces all physical symptoms. Physical illness represents a belief in magic. The whole distortion that made magic rests on the belief that there is a creative ability in matter which the mind cannot control. This error can take two forms; it can be believed that the mind can miscreate in the body, or that the body can miscreate in the mind. When it is understood that the mind, the only level of creation, cannot create beyond itself, neither type of confusion need occur." (2:5-10)

"All material means that you accept as remedies for bodily ills are restatements of magic principles. This is the first step in believing that the body makes its own illness. It is a second misstep to attempt to heal it through non-creative agents. It does not follow, however, that the use of such agents for corrective purposes is evil. Sometimes the illness has a sufficiently strong hold over the mind to render a person temporarily inaccessible to the Atonement. In this case it may be wise to utilize a compromise approach to mind and body, in which something from the outside is temporarily given healing belief." (4:1-6)

ME: Okay, so all illness is a result of our own misdirected thoughts about Who We Are. This error; the belief that we are a body and at the mercy of it; is at the root of all forms of sickness?

HS: Correct. In answer to your question about whether or not you are perpetuating the illusion through your chosen line of work as a pharmacist, the answer is: No. No line of work in the world is more or less holy or spiritual than another. When performed with a mindset of love and helpfulness, all professions equally guide you Home. It doesn't matter if you clean bathrooms, wait on tables, or dispense medications for a living. Do your job with dignity, grace, and love for others, and you will bring healing to the world in whatever you do.

ME: Alright. I have another question along the lines of healing. Is it okay to pray to You for help in healing? I mean, you make it sound as though it's all my own responsibility because all my problems are caused by my thoughts. But I don't feel comfortable with that. You could say that thought *increases my fear.*

HS: Of course it's appropriate to pray to Me for healing. In fact, there is no other way to *be* healed except through Me. However, most people don't understand the most effective way to pray for healing. There is a way to consciously and knowingly open up and allow My intervention.

ME: Well I'd love to know how to do that. Please do share.

HS: Look in the section of the ACIM titled, "The Song of Prayer." You will find it there.

The following quotation from the Course is from SONG OF PRAYER Chapter 3 — IV. The Holiness of Healing

"You first forgive, then pray, and you are healed. Your prayer has risen up and called to God, Who hears and answers. You have understood that you forgive and pray but for yourself. And in this understanding you are healed. In prayer you have united with your Source, and understood that you have never left. This level cannot be attained until there is no hatred in your heart, and no desire to attack the Son of God." (4:1-6)

ME: So all prayer must begin with forgiveness for myself?

HS: Correct. When you pray, it must always be first for yourself. Always your prayer must be to see yourself and those around you correctly; as One United Love. Without this, your prayer is of the ego, and My answer will always be one that directs you away from the ego. This is why so many think their prayers go unanswered. I *always* answer, but with the answer that is best for you. There can be no healing until you let go of all thoughts of fear, hatred and attack towards others. Those who are unhealed themselves, cannot hope to bring healing to others. Pray first, to see everything in the world as I do; with equal, and unconditional love and trust. Pray to see whomever you see as experiencing bodily suffering, as *not* a body. There is nothing to fear, because no one is in danger. In this way, you step aside and allow My grace to enter and heal you both.

ME: Okay, but it's hard to pray without fear. Fear is the whole reason I'm praying to You to begin with! Let's say I'm worried about a sick loved one and I want to help them heal. How should I pray to heal them? I guess what I'm asking is, how do we learn to heal the way Jesus healed people? I know this is possible. He said so Himself.

HS: Please share here the TEXT section that concerns your question.

**The following quotations from the Course are from
TEXT Chapter 27 — V. The Healing Example**

"The only way to heal is to be healed." (1:1)

"No one can ask another to be healed. But he can let *himself*
be healed, and thus offer the other what he has received. Who
can bestow upon another what he does not have? And who
can share what he denies himself? The Holy Spirit speaks to
you. He does not speak to someone else. Yet by your listening
His Voice extends, because you have accepted what He says."
(1:6-12)

"No one is healed through double messages. If you wish
only to be healed, you heal. Your single purpose makes this
possible. But if you are afraid of healing, then it cannot come
through you. The only thing that is required for a healing is a
lack of fear." (2:4-8)

"This does not mean the conflict must be gone forever from
your mind to heal." (2:10)

"But it does mean, if only for an instant, you love without
attack. An instant is sufficient. Miracles wait not on time."
(2:12-14)

"The holy instant is the miracle's abiding place. From there,
each one is born into this world as witness to a state of mind
that has transcended conflict, and has reached to peace." (3:1-
2)

"Problems are not specific but they take specific forms,
and these specific shapes make up the world. And no one
understands the nature of his problem. If he did, it would be
there no more for him to see." (8:1-3)

"But healing is apparent in specific instances, and generalizes
to include them all. This is because they really are the same,
despite their different forms." (8:6-7)

"Your healing will extend, and will be brought to problems

that you thought were not your own." (9:1)

"Leave, then, the transfer of your learning to the One Who really understands its laws, and Who will guarantee that they remain unviolated and unlimited. Your part is merely to apply what He has taught you to yourself, and He will do the rest." (10:1-2)

"Each one may seem to have a problem that is different from the rest. Yet they are solved together. And their common answer shows the questions could not have been separate." (10:5-7)

"And you will learn that peace is given you when you accept the healing for yourself." (11:2)

"Infinity cannot be understood by merely counting up its separate parts." (11:8)

ME: So let me get this straight. I cannot heal others, until I see all problems as the same problem, and have no fear of the outcome, trusting in the Love that unifies us all?

HS: Correct.

ME: And by healing, we're talking about healing our inner conflict first, right?

HS: Correct.

ME: So then it stands to reason that physical healing cannot take place until our own inner conflict is healed?

HS: You understand perfectly.

ME: But it's not necessary that we walk around all saintly and peaceful all the time, right? We just have to know *for a holy instant* that we are at one with everyone else, and united by the same Love. Right?

HS: You've got it.

ME: Okay, so now something from the bible has just popped into my head. I can't emphasize enough how weird this is for me, because I've been sort of an anti-bible person for many years now. To even bring up references to it is difficult for me. So I know this is Your doing. That being said, what is it You want to talk about regarding Jesus healing the blind man by placing mud on his eyes? I don't remember much about this story, so I suppose I'm going to have to look it up on the internet.

HS: Please do. Then come back here and discuss it with Me. I don't need you to quote it exactly, just give a brief summary and the bible reference.

ME: Alright. I read it. It's found in John 9:1-12. So to sum it up, Jesus saw a man alongside the road who had been born blind. He then made some mud using His own spit and some clay from the ground at His feet, and plastered it over the man's eyes. Jesus then told the man to go wash it off in a nearby pool. After the man did this, his eyes could see.

HS: And why do you think Jesus did this?

ME: Ah ha... I am beginning to see something here too... Jesus used a combination of "medicine" and spiritual healing to heal the man's eyes. Why did He do that? Clearly He didn't need to, right?

HS: Jesus healed the man in this way due to his lack of faith, and fear of his own healing. Jesus knew that applying mud to the man's eyes was a healing method he could accept with the least amount of fear. There was nothing curative about the clay itself, or the saliva of Jesus. The man had to fearlessly believe in his own healing in order for the miracle to be accepted. The mud simply helped him believe he could be healed, and that was all.

ME: And so I see how prayer, traditional medicine, and faith all converge to bring about healing in the physical. First I must have faith in the peace of Christ within myself, before I can extend it to others. This can be achieved through whatever means I'm most able to accept without fear.

HS: You are seeing correctly. Understand that all healing follows from your acceptance of My stillness and peace within yourself.

168

Chapter 23: Lessons 291-300

Death, Loss and Pain

Lesson 291. This is a day of stillness and of peace.

HS: Stillness and peace cannot come to you while you hold hands with the ego. When your peace is disturbed in any way, you can be sure it is of the ego. Let forgiveness peacefully lay these thoughts to rest in stillness and peace. Despite what your fears may be, a happy outcome to all things is sure.

292. A happy outcome to all things is sure.

HS: Know that a happy outcome to all your problems is assured. However, while you think the ego can bring you what you want, happiness will escape you. Yet, God has promised that you will not have to wait forever. Nothing can prevent God's Will from being done on earth. All things you now perceive as "problems" will have a happy ending. Have faith that all fear is past and only love is here.

293. All fear is past and only love is here.

HS: The ego has no hold on you. You are entirely safe in the present moment. To be fully in the present moment, is forgiveness. It is a state in which you have let all things be exactly as they are. You cannot live in two places at once. You must choose between the past or the present. When you are fully present, all is forgiven and fear is truly past; being both behind you, and gone. Your body and the past it holds, is nothing. Forgive the body. It is a wholly neutral thing.

294. My body is a wholly neutral thing.

HS: The body is a mask. When you are tempted to believe it is real, you must remember the one eternal truth about yourself: you are united in a holy relationship as God's One Son. Forget this, and you are thrown into darkness and illusion. The body is to be neither vilified nor exalted. Its only purpose, is to serve as your vehicle for forgiveness. It is a wholly neutral thing. You must see it as a window through which the Holy Spirit may look out of you.

295. The Holy Spirit looks through me today.

HS: When you choose to allow the Holy Spirit to look through your eyes, you will see a world forgiven of all its sin and separation. Through this way of seeing, the dream is slowly lifted from your sight. When you see the world as innocent, you can't help but see yourself as innocent along with it. You cannot be saved alone. It is through your willingness to see the sameness of God in all, that you are redeemed together. You appear as many forms, but you are each awakening to One Love. Accept this as your vision, and the Holy Spirit is allowed to speak to the world through you.

296. The Holy Spirit speaks through me today.

HS: My Voice cannot be heard without your being still and peaceful inside. My Voice cannot be heard above the loud complaints of the ego. I condemn no one, and neither should you. You have used God's power to hide the real world of Heaven, and so you have the power to reveal it once again; through forgiveness. This is the greatest gift you can bestow upon the world and your brethren. Forgiveness is the only gift you need give.

297. Forgiveness is the only gift I give.

HS: What you give, is what you receive. This is the Law of Love, the Law of Life and the Law of God. Some have called it the Law of Attraction. It cannot be escaped. Therefore, let forgiveness be the only gift you give, for it is the only thing you need. Giving and receiving are the same, because you are One in God. You cannot love your Father, without also loving His Son.

298. I love You, Father, and I love Your Son.

HS: You cannot see what lies behind the body. Because of this, you can hardly be blamed for forgetting your love for one another; for failing at times to treat each other with kindness. Accept instead only what God has established as yours; your holy Sonship in Him. You must learn to walk through this world of illusion, knowing that eternal holiness abides in each of you.

299. Eternal holiness abides in me.

HS: The body fills your senses and it can be difficult to see yourself as anything else. But God has not forgotten the eternal holiness abiding in you.

His senses are not clouded. He sees only the truth in you. Your holiness cannot be undone. God Wills that you remember the holiness He created you as. Once you remember this, then only an instant longer will this world endure for you.

300. Only an instant does this world endure.

HS: This statement brings great sadness to those who hold tightly to the ego, hoping to find happiness in this world. For those who are seeking release from pain, they are words of a glad release; the happy promise of eternal joy. There is nothing here in the world that you can take with you into the Kingdom of Heaven, because none of it is real. Only the Eternal Holiness abiding within you is real, and this alone is welcomed into His Kingdom. The holy instant you accept this truth, the world as you know it will cease to endure and you will move beyond it to eternity.

• • •

ME: When You talk about us moving beyond this world to eternity, are You talking about our physical death?

HS: No. I am talking about your true Life in Spirit. I am talking about a shift in your perception; a shift in awareness. It is a shift from seeing this world; the world you made in opposition to Me; to seeing My world. The world I created is the only real world there is. The world you currently see was born of sacrifice. You have sacrificed your Perfect Vision of Oneness in order to experience this illusion of separation. Please insert-

ME: I got it, I got it. Intuitive quote fetching person at Your service.

The following quotations from the Course are from TEXT Chapter 26 — I. The "Sacrifice" of Oneness

"The world you see is based on "sacrifice" of oneness. It is a picture of complete disunity and total lack of joining. Around each entity is built a wall so seeming solid that it looks as if what is inside can never reach without, and what is out can never reach and join with what is locked away within the wall.

Each part must sacrifice the other part, to keep itself complete. For if they joined each one would lose its own identity, and by their separation are their selves maintained." (2:1-5)

"The body *is* a loss, and *can* be made to sacrifice. And while you see your brother as a body, apart from you and separate in his cell, you are demanding sacrifice of him and you." (4:1-2)

"You can lose sight of oneness, but can not make sacrifice of its reality. Nor can you lose what you would sacrifice, nor keep the Holy Spirit from His task of showing you that it has not been lost." (6:1-2)

ME: Okay, so we "sacrificed" our vision of Oneness in order to experience being in separate bodies, but in reality, we are One, whether we see bodies or not.

HS: Correct.

ME: But the body *can* be lost, and even though we aren't supposed to see one another as a body, it still hurts like hell when a loved one is lost. So will You please explain to me how we're supposed to deal with the emotional pain of death in light of our Oneness?

HS: I would love to.

ME: And You know what else hurts? The ending of a relationship. Sometimes that can hurt just as much as death, so I'd like to know how we should deal with that as well. I mean, losing someone is losing someone, right?

HS: Most certainly.

ME: And don't just say that bodies aren't real so we should just forgive them and let go of the pain. It's not that simple to do during the throws of agony. That thought isn't really helpful when we first experience the death or loss of someone, if You know what I mean?

HS: I promise I will not just tell you to forgive the body and let it go.

ME: Good. Alright then. Go ahead, I'm listening.

HS: First, I will address your question about how to deal with the pain of losing a loved one to death of the body. I will explain this through a brief exercise.

ME: Alright. That sounds fun.

HS: I want you to stop and take a moment to touch your own arm. It feels as though it is the real you, does it not?

ME: Yes, my skin feels like it's part of me.

HS: Now imagine yourself touching someone else's body with yours; someone you love very much. Imagine holding them in a deep, tender, loving embrace. Perhaps you caress their face, and give their cheek a gentle kiss. Now simply rest your forehead against theirs.

ME: Got it. I'm imagining that I'm holding and loving my two children. I'm really enjoying this exercise so far by the way.

HS: Good. Now, you feel such love for them, and they are dear to you. Under these circumstances, you feel supremely close to them, do you not?

ME: Yes, I feel very close to them like this.

HS: Now. I'm going to tell you something very important. Pay close attention.

ME: I'm totally listening here. I'm literally hanging off the edge of my seat. I'm not even breathing.

HS: This tender embrace is as *far apart as you will ever be* from those whom you hold dear. This is as far away from one another as you can possibly get. Nothing separates you more than the flesh. Physical bodies are a very real barrier to you.

ME: What? But if one of my children were to die, they would suddenly feel extremely far away from me. I don't ever want that.

HS: I tell you this; though you would miss their face, their touch, and the sound of their voice, you are never as far apart as you are now while you think you are in bodies. Nothing is closer than Oneness in My Spirit, and nothing separates you more than this dream of being in a body. As you are now, you are as far away from your loved ones as you will ever be. Once one of you departs from the physical, the rejoining process begins. You cannot see them, but they are there, waiting for your imminent return, knowing your seeming separation is but an instant in eternity. Upon your happy return, you will be together forever. You will never feel this much space between you again.

ME: At least not until we decide to come back here into bodies and forget everything again.

HS: Who says you have to return? It is My goal to help you to cease making the choice of separation to begin with.

ME: Oh yeah. I'd love to stop doing that.

HS: You never knew you had a choice until now.

ME: Right. And I want to point something out to You now; You *did* actually tell me the body isn't real, and we should forgive it. You just used a roundabout way to do it.

HS: I did not go back on my word. I gave you no trifle thing here. The pain of loss will heal of its own accord when the body is properly perceived.

ME: I believe You. Yes, You gave me new perspective beautifully, and I thank You. It's comforting to know that this is as far away as I will ever be from those I love.

HS: You are only dreaming of death. It is not a real experience. You never leave anyone, and no one ever leaves you.

The following quotations from the Course are from
MANUAL FOR TEACHERS
27. What Is Death?

"Death is the central dream from which all illusions stem. Is it not madness to think of life as being born, aging, losing vitality, and dying in the end?" (1:1-2)

"In this perception of the universe as God created it, it would be impossible to think of Him as loving. For who has decreed that all things pass away, ending in dust and disappointment and despair, can but be feared." (2:1-2)

"Death is the symbol of the fear of God." (3:1)

"The "reality" of death is firmly rooted int he belief that God's Son is a body. And if God created bodies, death would indeed be real. But God would not be loving." (5:1-3)

"Without the idea of death there is no world. All dreams will end with this one. This is salvation's final goal; the end of all Illusions." (6:3-5)

"Teacher of God, your one assignment could be stated thus: Accept no compromise in which death plays a part. Do not believe in cruelty, nor let attack conceal the truth from you. What seems to die has but been misperceived and carried to illusion. Now it becomes your task to let the illusion be carried to the truth. Be steadfast but in this; be not deceived by the "reality" of any changing form. Truth neither moves nor wavers nor sinks down to death and dissolution. And what is the end of death? Nothing but this; the realization that the Son of God is guiltless now and forever. Nothing but this. But do not let yourself forget it is not less than this." (7:1-10)

HS: The body is an illusion of changing form and nothing more. It is not real; it is not you. The death of it is nothing, because the body is indeed truly nothing. Though the loss of it grieves you, understand no one has gone anywhere except to exit the dream they were a body. Simultaneously rejoice in their freedom from hell.

ME: A while back, I had a dream about losing all my loved ones. I went out looking for them, thinking everyone had abandoned me. After I grew tired of looking for them, I decided to return home. Once

I got back, I found they'd all been at home waiting for me the whole time. It turned out that *I* was actually the one who'd left *them*.

HS: Each one of you is truly a prodigal son. It is the truth that *you* have actually left *them*. Heaven is your true Home, and this dream is the place you have journeyed to. Yet no one has really gone anywhere. No one has been lost or stolen from you. You are all still together, no matter what your external circumstances appear to look like. All you need do is follow My gentle path of ease and light to return to them. Upon your return, you will find that your loved ones have been waiting for you this entire time. Here, when there is a death, you think the person has left you, but you have the process backwards. Death of the body is actually the beginning of the return journey Home to Me. And I walk with you every step of the way. Do not fear this transition.

The following quotations from the Course are from TEXT Chapter 18 — III. Light in the Dream

"If you knew Who walks beside you on the way that you have chosen, fear would be impossible. You do not know because the journey into darkness has been long and cruel, and you have gone deep into it." (3:2-3)

"When you retreat to the illusion your fear increases, for there is little doubt that what you think it means *is* fearful. Yet what is that to us who travel surely and very swiftly away from fear?" (3:8-9)

"You do not understand what you accepted, but remember that your understanding is not necessary. All that was necessary was merely the *wish* to understand. That wish was the desire to be holy. The Will of God is granted you. For you desire the only thing you ever had, or ever were." (4:11-15)

"Your desire is now in complete accord with all the power of the Holy Spirit's Will." (5:3)

"I hold your hand as surely as you agreed to take your brother's. You will not separate, for I stand with you and walk with you in your advance to truth. And where we go we carry God with us." (5:5-7)

"Let not time worry you, for all the fear that you and your brother experience is really past. Time has been readjusted to help us do, together, what your separate pasts would hinder." (7:5-6)

"You and your brother are coming home together, after a long and meaningless journey that you undertook apart, and that lead nowhere. You have found your brother, and you will light each other's way." (8:5-6)

ME: That all sounds very nice, but while we're still stuck here, it sucks to feel left behind. Is it alright to grieve for those we've lost? I mean, You don't expect us to be happy about them returning Home, do You?

HS: Of course not. Grieving is a natural part of the healing process. You cannot accept what you do not acknowledge. Accept and acknowledge your losses in the way that's most comfortable for you, for the length of time you need. Just know, that one day you will rejoice in your holy Union once again. A Union more complete and loving than you have words on earth to describe. All suffering will be forgotten as the separation of the body is forgotten.

ACIM Preface xii.

"Only minds can really join, and whom God has joined no man can put asunder. It is, however, only at the level of Christ Mind that true union is possible, and has, in fact, never been lost."

ME: I love the idea of being One with everyone and that we never truly separate. Believing this takes some of the sting out of death I guess. Can You explain to me now how we should deal with the ending of relationships? It's not quite the same as death, but it can feel just as painful.

HS: Again, all you need is the proper perspective of what a body is *for* in a relationship in order to bring healing.

ME: Well, it's for loving the other person, isn't it?

HS: Close. It is for creating peace. The goal of every relationship, is *peace*. Once you have peace, the relationship manifests happiness, joy, and love. Where there is no peace, there is no love. And peace can be found whether bodies are together or not. It is up to you to decide under what circumstances peace is attained.

ME: Um, what?

HS: Peace cannot be found while you hold the body responsible for your happiness. Therefore, the body must sometimes be removed from your sight, in order to see My Spirit within them. You must therefore give all your relationships to Me, and I will make them holy. This may sometimes appear to be a painful process of separation, but do not fear this transition. I will bring you peace whether bodies are together or not. It is through the healing of all your special love and special hate relationships- those relationships where you treat another with "special" feelings- that you will come to remember My peace.

The following quotations from the Course are from TEXT Chapter 16 — IV. The Illusion and the Reality of Love

"Be not afraid to look upon the special hate relationship, for freedom lies in looking at it. It would be impossible not to know the meaning of love, except for this. For the special love relationship, in which the meaning of love is hidden, is undertaken solely to offset the hate, but not to let it go. Your salvation will rise clearly before your open eyes as you look on this." (1:1-4)

"The symbols of hate against the symbols of love play out a conflict that does not exist." (2:1)

"You will go through this last undoing quite unharmed, and will at last emerge as yourself. This is the last step in the readiness for God. Be not unwilling now; you are too near, and you will cross the bridge in perfect safety, translated quietly from war to peace." (2:3-5)

"The special love relationship is an attempt to limit the destructive effects of hate by finding a haven in the storm of guilt." (3:1)

"The special love relationship is not perceived as a value in itself, but as a place of safety from which hatred is split off and kept apart. The special love partner is acceptable only as long as he serves this purpose. Hatred can enter, and indeed is welcome in some aspects of the relationship, but it is still held together by the illusion of love. If the illusion goes, the relationship is broken or becomes unsatisfying on the grounds of disillusionment." (3:4-7)

"It is sure that those who select certain ones as partners in any aspect of living, and use them for any purpose which they would not share with others, are trying to live with guilt rather than die of it." (4:5)

"They seek it desperately, but not in the peace in which it would gladly come quietly to them. And when they find the fear of death is still upon them, the love relationship loses the illusion that it is what it is not." (5:4-5)

"Your task is not to seek for love, but merely to seek and find all of the barriers within yourself that you have built against. It." (6:1)

"Every illusion is one of fear, whatever form it takes. And the attempt to escape from one illusion into another must fail. If you seek love outside yourself you can be certain that you perceive hatred within, and are afraid of it." (6.:3-5)

"Recognize this, for it is true, and truth must be recognized if it is to be distinguished from illusion: The special love relationship is an attempt to bring love into separation." (7:1)

"It is essential that we look very closely at exactly what it is you think you can do to solve the dilemma which seems very real to you, but which does not exist. You have come close to truth, and only this stands between you and the bridge that leads you into it." (7:5-6)

"Across the bridge is your completion, for you will be wholly in God, willing for nothing special, but only to be wholly like to Him, completing Him by your completion." (9:1)

"Seek not for this in the bleak world of illusion, where nothing is certain and where everything fails to satisfy. In the Name of God, be wholly willing to abandon all illusions." (9:4-5)

"Every fantasy, be it of love or hate, deprives you of knowledge for fantasies are the veil behind which truth is hidden." (10:3)

"The journey that seemed endless is almost complete, for what is endless is very near. You have almost recognized it. Turn with me firmly away from all illusions now, and let nothing stand in the way of truth. We will take the last useless journey away from truth together, and then together we go straight to God, in joyous answer to His Call for His completion." (12:3-6)

ME: Ah. So as long as we continue to see relationships between bodies as the source of our happiness, we are only perpetuating the illusion. We cannot place the duty of our happiness on others. In this illusion we promise to love someone, but only as long as the person does what we want. Once the other person deviates from our rules for happiness in a relationship, it turns to hate. We get mad at them, and our special love relationship turns to a special hate relationship. We then sometimes decide to physically separate. Right?

HS: Correct. A relationship not at peace, is painful. No one enjoys this type of situation. It is up to you how peace is restored. You can decide to have peace *with* the other person, or *without* them. Either way, you must let go of all thoughts of conflict about them. Forget that they are a body. You must let go of the idea that their bodily presence and actions are the source of your happiness. The source of your happiness is your Union in peace with them through Me. Nothing else will bring you happiness.

ME: I'll need to practice thinking like that. I have one more question about pain. What about physical pain? Is there a special way we should see that too?

HS: Yes. Physical pain is strongly linked to physical pleasure, and they are both demonstrations of your belief in sin- the error in belief you are a body.

The following quotations from the Course are from TEXT Chapter 27 — VI. The Witnesses to Sin

"Pain demonstrates the body must be real. It is a loud, obscuring voice whose shrieks would silence what the Holy Spirit says, and keep His words from your awareness. Pain compels attention, drawing it away from Him and focusing upon itself. Its purpose is the same as pleasure, for they both are means to make the body real." (1:1-4)

"Pleasure and pain are equally unreal, because their purpose cannot be achieved." (1:7)

"Sin shifts from pain to pleasure, and again to pain. For either witness is the same, and carries but one message: "You are here, within this body, and you can be hurt. You can have pleasure, too, but only at the cost of pain."" (2:1-3)

"This body, purposeless within itself, holds all your memories and all your hopes. You use its eyes to see, its ears to hear, and let it tell you what it feels. *It does not know.*" (3:1-3)

"Each miracle He brings is witness that the body is not real. Its pains and pleasures does He heal alike, for all sin's witnesses do His replace." (4:8-9)

"It matters not the name by which you called your suffering. It is no longer there. The One Who brings the miracle perceives them all as one, and called by name of fear." (5:4-6)

"Yet to the One Who sends forth miracles to bless the world, a tiny stab of pain, a little worldly pleasure, and the throes of death itself are but a single sound; a call for healing, and a plaintive cry for help within a world of misery." (6:6)

"There is no need to suffer any more. But there *is* need that you be healed, because the suffering and sorrow of the world have made it deaf to its salvation and deliverance." (7:2-3)

"Offer the miracle of the holy instant through the Holy Spirit, and leave His giving it to you to Him." (15:1)

ME: So all forms of pain and pleasure are really just one big distraction? It's the ego trying to demonstrate to us that we are a body and not Spirit? How do we overcome this?

HS: *You* don't overcome anything by yourself. I take care of your pain through your relinquishment of it to Me in the holy instant. All pain will cease the moment you choose to be healed, and you choose healing through forgiveness of sin.

ME: And sin is the error of belief we are a body. Gah! That's so hard to remember!

HS: Just remember that all pain is simply a cry for help; be it your pain, or someone else's. It's all the same cry for release from this illusion, and whatever form the pain takes, it all requires the same answer: You are My holy Son, and I am your Father. Be healed of all pain through forgiving what you are not, and acceptance of Who You Are.

ME: That sounds easier said than done.

HS: Indeed, and I restate that you cannot do it alone. I am here to help you. I have come to wipe away all your tears.

Chapter 24: Lessons 301-310

We're Doing This to Ourselves

301. And God Himself shall wipe away all tears.

HS: Every tear you experience is at your own hands. You suffer needlessly. To end your suffering, you must suspend all judgement, and exhibit true forgiveness instead. Once all judgements are laid aside, God Himself will wipe away all your tears, as you look upon what God Created rather than what your ego made. Where darkness once was, you will look upon the light.

302. Where darkness was I look upon the light.

HS: You know from your own experience that you cannot see both darkness and light simultaneously. Turn on a light switch, and know the truth in this. Neither can you see both illusion and truth simultaneously. Fear and Love cannot coexist. They cannot occupy the same space within your mind. Choose the light, by choosing to forgive the world you see now. This choice opens a door within you; a shaft of light into a dark room; as you invite Christ to enter. Open the door to Christ through your thoughts of peace, so that He may walk out upon the world, correcting what you made. In this way, Christ is born in you.

303. The holy Christ is born in me today.

HS: Christ is born in you through your inner stillness. Christ is welcomed within you, through the peace of your forgivenesses. He *is* peace. You have forgotten that you are also His peace. Forget the ego and remember instead your true Identity. You cannot be two identities at the same time. You cannot serve two masters. Let not your world obscure the sight of Christ.

304. Let not my world obscure the sight of Christ.

HS: The outer world is a reflection of your inner state. It's darkness literally mirrors what you believe to be true about yourself. Yet, Christ will lead you out of all darkness and illusion to your holiness. The clear sight of truth that your forgiveness blesses the world with, brings a peace that only Christ can bestow on you.

305. There is a peace that Christ bestows on us.

HS: True forgiveness does not look at the *form* surrounding Life, but acknowledges only the light *within* the form. Every person you interact with during your daily life or think about within your mind, has been sent to you as a gift. They are a gift, because if you can manage to see past their form; past all the aggravations, pain, and suffering they seem to bring you; you will experience deep peace in knowing you are all equal in God's Love. To see past these differences is a gift of peace from Christ. The gift of Christ is all you seek.

306. The gift of Christ is all I seek today.

HS: Christ looks upon the world and sees only Unity. His Vision of peace must be all you seek, for it means the end of your forgiveness lessons. It means you are on the cusp of the Second Coming and the return of your forgotten memories of God. There is no greater gift than to be redeemed and born again into the loving kindness and peace of God. While conflict yet remains within you, you cannot accept His gift. Do you want conflict, or the peace of God? Conflicting wishes cannot be your will.

307. Conflicting wishes cannot be my will.

HS: There is a constant battle going on within you between the ego and the Holy Spirit. It is not a two-way battle. The ego attacks and judges, while the Holy Spirit simply does not respond. The truth needs no defense. It is insane to think you want conflict over the peace of God. Until this conflict is settled, you must constantly choose between the ego and God's Will. His Will is your Unity. The moment you join God's Will by laying down the past, you instantly enter a present state of peace. This instant is the only time there is.

308. This instant is the only time there is.

HS: Time is actually for learning to be in the present moment. The present moment is the only real time there is. The past and future do not exist. Christ's Love is ever present within you, in the present. You have been looking for Him everywhere, watching for outward signs. He will not return through the illusion of this world. He will come again only through that part of you which is real; your true Self, that lies *within*. Do not fear to look within.

309. I will not fear to look within today.

HS: You fear to look within, because you know you will see a contradiction between what your ego shows you, and who you are in truth. Currently, you see your Self as fractured into a million different pieces, each separated by a body, when in truth You are all God's One Son. Do not fear to see this truth within your brothers and yourself. Live in fearlessness and love.

310. In fearlessness and love I spend today.

HS: This world of separation was made through your fear. To be fearless then, is to have forgiven the world and dare to see the love that lies beneath it instead. Once you do this, you will experience a world of peace. Fear has no place in a world where you are all One. There is nothing to fear when all things are seen as Whole.

· · ·

ME: I want to go back to lesson 301, where You said, "every tear you experience is at your own hands." I still resist the idea that I'm solely responsible for all the bad stuff that happens to me. I understand You've tried to explain to me that my thoughts create my reality, but *I really don't want pain*. So what gives? What am I missing here?

HS: What I am trying to teach here, is not just a simple mantra that "your thoughts create your reality." That is what many of the New Age teachings of the Law of Attraction preach. What I am trying to establish, is an entirely new thought system. I am teaching you how to turn your entire mind over to God, and in order to do that, you must understand how to release yourself to Him. You must come to understand that you are the source of your own pain. No one else is doing this to you. Until this is understood, you will be held hostage by your own dream of pain.

**The following quotations from the Course are from
TEXT Chapter 27 — VIII. The "Hero" of the Dream**

"The body is the central figure of the dreaming world." (1:1)

"The dreaming of the world takes many forms, because the body seeks in many ways to prove it is autonomous and real." (2:1)

"The body's serial adventures, from the time of birth to dying are the theme of every dream the world has ever had." (3:1)

"Thus are you not the dreamer, but the dream. And so you wander idly in and out of places and events that it contrives. That is all the body does is true, for it is but a figure in a dream." (4:1-3)

"The instant that he sees them as they are they have no more effects on him, because he understands he gave them their effects by causing them and making them seem real." (4:5)

"Then let us merely look upon the dream's beginning, for the part you see is but the second part, whose cause lies in the first. No one asleep and dreaming in the world remembers his attack upon himself. No one believes there really was a time when he knew nothing of a body, and could never have conceived this world as real." (5:3-5)

"The world you see depicts exactly what you thought you did. Except that now you think that what you did is being done to you. The guilt for what you thought is being placed outside yourself, and on a guilty world that dreams your dreams and thinks your thoughts instead of you. It brings its vengeance, not your own." (7:2-5)

"Perhaps you come in tears. But hear Him say, "My brother, holy Son of God, behold your idle dream, in which this could occur." And you will leave the holy instant with your laughter and your brother's joined with His." (9:6-8)

"The secret of salvation is but this: that you are doing this unto yourself. No matter what the form of the attack, this still is true." (10:1-2)

"This single lesson learned will set you free from suffering whatever form it takes. The Holy Spirit will repeat this one inclusive lesson of deliverance until it has been learned, regardless of the form of suffering that brings you pain." (11:1-2)

"Salvation is a secret you have kept but from yourself." (12:4)

"When you forgive the world your guilt, you will be free of it." (13:2)

"And it is this that has maintained you separate from the world, and kept your brother separate from you. Now need you but to learn that both of you are innocent or guilty. The one thing that is impossible is that you be unlike each other; that they both be true. This is the only secret yet to learn. And it will be no secret you are healed." (13:5-9)

HS: To clarify this; as long as you believe yourself to be separate from everyone else, you will remain asleep. This one thought, corrected, will bring you to the holy instant; the instant of your salvation from this world. You will be saved from the dream of pain and death.

ME: So the instant I see myself as one with my brother, I will be released from this world and see Heaven instead?

HS: Correct. I know you are thinking that you *already* believe and understand that you're one with everyone. That's a good starting place. Know it in your mind at first, but then begin to hold it there throughout each day. The moment you forget, and slip into discomfort, remind yourself that none of what you see is your Real Home. You need not have perfect thoughts every second. All you need to do is remember to let them go as they arise. In this way, the world is healed through one forgiving thought at a time. Everything you see is sin; an error. Therefore, judge nothing, knowing you do not see things as they are in truth.

Chapter 25: Lessons 311-320

Unfairness

311. I judge all things as I would have them be.

HS: What you would judge to be a body, will appear to you as a body. Judge your brother as Christ, and you will see Him. Your eyes deceive you and you do not know you look upon God's Son. Instead, you see all things as you *think* you would have them be.

312. I see all things as I would have them be.

HS: You *see* what you *think*. You do not consider the possibility that your thoughts have the power to manifest your reality. Yet, it is true. It is Christ's gift to you. Know that you have the ability to change your mind, and change what you see. Now let a new perception come to you.

313. Now let a new perception come to me.

HS: What is this new perception? It is a perception that sees no illusion. It is to see with Christ's Vision and behold a forgiven world. This new perception brings with it the Last Judgment; the final judgment upon the world that all sins are forgiven. From this thought forward, you will see a new reality. It is this reality you seek, and it is much different from your past.

314. I seek a future different from the past.

HS: The future you experience is projected from your present thoughts. Therefore, you must have thoughts of forgiveness *now* in order to see a future blessed with it. Every time you look upon your brothers, you have an opportunity to see them differently. You have an opportunity to forgive what is false. As you bless your brothers with forgiveness, their forgiveness is returned to you. This gift they give belongs to you.

315. All gifts my brothers give belong to me.

HS: What gifts do your brothers give? They give you the opportunity to love them as they truly are, and in return, you will know yourself as you truly are.

With deepest gratitude, accept the gifts each of your brothers offer you, and as you accept them, you make these gifts your own.

316. All gifts I give my brothers are my own.

HS: There is no greater gift than to remember your Oneness. Extend this gift to your brothers, and it is yours as well. As you remember this, you follow in the way appointed you.

317. I follow in the way appointed me.

HS: God has appointed your way, but He will not force you to follow Him in it. God will allow you to remain in time, living incarnation after incarnation in a human body, until you decide to leave the dream at last. Forgiving the illusion of this world and following Him to salvation is His Way. In you, salvation's means and end are one.

318. In me salvation's means and end are one.

HS: It is with your decision to forgive that salvation comes. You must recognize that Christ stands before you each time you look upon your brothers. You must meet all things that arise before your eyes with instant and complete forgiveness. Your recognition of Love within all people, is both salvation's means and end. Salvation is but to recognize your Unity and Oneness. This is what each of you has come here to do; salvage your seemingly separated parts. You came for the salvation of the world.

319. I came for the salvation of the world.

HS: You are salvaged through the recognition of your Unity. Only the ego seeks to be alone, separate, and "special." Only the ego believes that some of you are "better" or "more qualified" to do what you have each come here to do. It is God's Will that you each bring salvation to the world, but in order for this to happen, your love must become all inclusive. There can be no exclusions. To have, you must give all to all. This is the power your Father gives you.

320. My Father gives all power unto me.

HS: This power is real. It is no trifle thing, and should not be cast aside lightly. The power you have been given will change the very fabric of the universe as you now see it. It is the power to heal the world through your forgiveness of it.

• • •

ME: Alright. I can believe God loves us all equally. I really can. I also believe in the power He gave us to change our reality through loving and forgiving all form we see. I really want to do that. The problem is, I often have trouble with it. For instance, I had a small upset with one of my coworkers two days ago. And I can't believe these tiny things still make me mad, given what I know now. But they do. I have trouble remembering what You've told me "in the heat of the moment" if You know what I mean.

HS: I understand. Why don't you share your story here, so that others may understand as well.

ME: Okay. So anyway, I was sitting at work with a bunch of stuff in front of me to do, but I took a moment to check my phone. My son had texted, and since it was a day he and his sister would be home alone after school for an hour, I took a minute to read and respond to it. It was at this moment a particularly obnoxious coworker saw my pile of work, and me on my phone. She assumed I was goofing off, and proceeded to make a rude comment to me about it. My anger went from zero to ten in less than a heartbeat. It was as though I had no control over my emotions. My only comment in return was that I was taking care of my children, but inside, I was seething! I really wanted to tell her off! About a hundred terrible replies went through my mind all at once. How should I have handled this? I know Christ is within every person, but I fail to remember it when people act rudely. In fact, it's been two days now, and if I allow myself to think about it, I get upset all over again. I can't seem to let it go, and it's such a small thing!

HS: My dear child, yours is a common problem that plagues the majority continuously. Here is what you must know in order to realize, at all times, that the Father, Son, and Holy Spirit reside within all whom you interact. To see Their Presence, you must let go of the notion that you can be unfairly treated.

The following quotations from the Course are from TEXT Chapter 26 — X. The End of Injustice

"What, then, remains to be undone for you to realize Their Presence? Only this; you have a differential view of when attack is justified, and when you think it is unfair and not to be allowed. When you perceive it as unfair, you think that a response of anger now is just. And thus you see what is the same as different. Confusion is not limited. If it occurs at all it will be total. And its presence, in whatever form, will hide Their Presence." (1:7)

"What does it mean if you perceive attack in certain forms to be unfair to you? It means that there must be some forms in which you think it fair." (2:1-2)

"Unfairness and attack are one mistake, so firmly joined that where one is perceived the other must be seen. You cannot be unfairly treated. The belief that you are is but another form of the idea you are deprived by someone not yourself." (3:1-3)

"Yet it is you who ask this of yourself, in deep injustice to the Son of God. You have no enemy except yourself, and you are enemy indeed to him because you do not know him *as* yourself." (3:5-6)

"Beware the temptation to perceive yourself unfairly treated." (4:1)

"You think your brother is unfair to you because you think that one must be unfair to make the other innocent. And in this game do you perceive one purpose for your whole relationship. And this you seek to add unto the purpose given it. The Holy Spirit's purpose is to let the Presence of your holy Guests be known to you. And to this purpose nothing can be added, for the world is purposeless except for this." (5:1-5)

"If you perceive injustice anywhere, you need but say:

*By this do I deny the Presence of the Father and the Son. And I
would rather know of Them than see injustice, which Their Presence
shines away."* (6:5-7)

HS: There are times when you believe in the possibility that one of you
can be guilty, and the other innocent; one of you is attacking and the other
defending; one person is right, and the other wrong. This cannot be possible
if seen through the eyes of truth. Truth says, unfair treatment is impossible if
you are truly One. How can what is One, be unfairly treated? All that you do,
is done only to *yourself*.

ME: I see what You are saying. The fastest way to correct the illusion
of unfair treatment, is to remember that I am One with everyone else,
and that I'd rather see Them (the Father, Son and Holy Spirit) above
all else. But that's hard to put into practice when someone's up in your
face. Deep down, all I want to do is put them in their place.

HS: It is through looking at your hostility that you will remember your own
place.

The following quotations from the Course are from
TEXT Chapter 13 — III. The Fear of Redemption

"You are not seriously disturbed by your hostility. You keep it
hidden because you are more afraid of what it covers." (1:7-8)

"You are not really afraid of crucifixion. Your real terror is of
redemption." (1:10-11)

"Under the ego's dark foundation is the memory of God, and
it is of this that you are really afraid. For this memory would
instantly restore you to your proper place, and it is this place
that you have sought to leave. Your fear of attack is nothing
compared to your fear of love." (2:1-3)

"For still deeper than the ego's foundation, and much stronger
than it will ever be, is your intense and burning love of God,
and His for you. This is what you really want to hide." (2:8-9)

"In honesty, is it not harder for you to say "I love" than "I hate?" You associate love with weakness and hatred with strength, and your own real power seems to you as your real weakness." 3:1-3)

"You have built your whole insane belief system because you think you would be helpless in God's Presence, and you would save yourself from His Love because you think it would crush you into nothingness." (4:1)

"Therefore, you have used the world to cover your love, and the deeper you go into the blackness of the ego's foundation, the closer you come to the Love that is hidden there. *And it is this that frightens you.*" (4:4-5)

"Lay before His eternal sanity all your hurt, and let Him heal you. Do not leave any spot of pain hidden from His light, and search your mind carefully for any thoughts you may fear to uncover." (7:4-5)

"But exempt no one from your love, or you will be hiding a dark place in your mind where the Holy Spirit is not welcome. And thus you will exempt yourself from His healing power, for by not offering total love you will not be healed completely." (9:2-3)

HS: You must always try to forgive your brethren their form. When you call on Them through your remembrance of Their Presence within another, They will step forward and heal your anger, restoring your peace.

ME: Yes, but how should I have responded to this person's rude remarks? What should I have said to her? Am I expected to just take it in silence? Being silent isn't exactly one of my strongest attributes. I am not a doormat.

HS: In the instance of antagonism, it is best to mind one's own business.

ME: So I should've just told her to mind her own business?!

HS: No. I am saying that *you* should've minded your *own*. You forgot what your real business was, and fell into the illusion of being unfairly treated.

ME: Can You please remind me again what my *real* business is?

HS: Your business is forgiveness. You have no business doing anything else. You are an unfit judge of her because you do not see her as she truly is, and so you judge her incorrectly. You cannot see that she is unhappy with her life, and that her thoughts are dark and depressing most of the time. You cannot see that since she feels no control over her own life, she is trying to control you instead. She is projecting her unhappiness onto you, making you the cause of it. You could sense these wordless accusations behind her statement to you, and it triggered a cascade of guilty feelings and wrongdoing within you. So you reacted in defense and anger; making her accusations real to you. You accepted her judgment upon you, deciding it was the truth. This caused you to lose your peace.

ME: (Gasp!) Oh for goodness *sake*. When will I *remember* this?! How long will it take for me to remember to forgive first, and ask questions later?

HS: How long is an instant?

ME: Right. Got it. However, there is still the problem of what I should've said to her.

HS: You are not responsible for anyone else's happiness, and neither are you the *cause* of anyone's *un*happiness. The same thought should be applied to yourself when you feel accusatory towards others. They are not responsible for your happiness, and neither are they the cause of your unhappiness. The only cause for unhappiness is the illusion of your separation from one another; and the remedy is My peace. In other words, your happiness is actually *My* responsibility, but you must choose it in order for Me to give it to you. In light of this knowledge, you could've reminded yourself that the goal of any relationship is peace, which brings with it, happiness. You do not actually want conflict with anyone. You want their blessing. So you could've said, "Be at peace my friend. You are not angry for the reasons you think. I am here only to love you and be helpful to you."

ME: Um. Yeah. Well *that's* not happening.

HS: Remember that all attack is simply a cry for love. When others see you as the cause of their misery, give them what they truly want: love. It is always going to be the ego that responds first with attack and hate, but it is up to you to reverse this thinking with thoughts of love. While you still listen to the ego, hate will always be easier than love. See how quickly you condemn another; yet find it difficult to love them while you perceive yourself as a victim of unfair treatment? See how you are unable to let go of the past?

ME: I do.

HS: There is a peace and a power in letting go, and you fear it is weakness. If you let go, you fear someone else may win, and you will lose. You fear someone may "get by" with hurting you. But there is a deep peace and a great power in setting down the past. Step away from what brings you pain. You don't have to bear it. I will. Give it to Me, and be free. Feel the peace and power of letting go. In Me you have God's Strength.

ME: I never thought of letting go of the past as a power that I held. You're right. I always think that if I don't defend myself somehow, that I'm weak and letting someone walk all over me. But it's a powerful thing to set down the past.

HS: Indeed it is. Jesus was no doormat for laying down His life for you- His friends. He was not a victim, but a glorious example of unconditional love in His resurrection.

ME: Good point.

HS: No one can take your power from you. Remember that you're not a victim of anyone else's condemnation. They are part of you, and need your love, and when you give it, you will receive love in return. Always say within your mind when conflict arises, "Give me your blessing holy Son of God." These words will call Me forward within whomever is upsetting you, and I will rise up and heal you both. Let Me be your eyes that see, your Voice that speaks, and your ears that hear.

ME: Thank you. I'm feeling total peace over this situation now. Unhappiness has no root cause in the world. Unhappiness stems from our decision to separate from You. I've done nothing to no one, and they've done nothing to me. No one has been unfairly treated. I feel absolved of all guilt and wrongdoing, knowing we were just projecting our own guilt onto one another. *I am not the cause of anyone else's unhappiness.* That's such a revelation for me. It also feels good to realize that *I am not responsible for anyone else's happiness.* Nor are they responsible for mine. I feel so light and free now!

HS: Precisely. Peace feels like freedom and freedom lies in Me alone.

Chapter 26: Lessons 321-330

Who Are You Listening To?

321. Father, my freedom is in You alone.

HS: You seem to be in an impossible situation. How can you ever see beyond this dream, if *it* is all you see? Healing your mind seems unattainable. You have searched the world outside in vain for freedom, not knowing it lay directly within, where your Father is. Your freedom lies in joining with God's Will, and it is His Will that you return your awareness to Him. With gladness, give up this illusory world you made in exchange for Heaven. You can give up but what was never real.

322. I can give up but what was never real.

HS: This world is not real, because it is not eternal. You can give up your body, but not your spirit. Your spirit cannot be changed, because God is unchangeable. You have only sacrificed your awareness of your eternal qualities through choosing to see separation. Now make a different choice. Choose to "sacrifice" fear in glad exchange for your reality in God's Love.

323. I gladly make the "sacrifice" of fear.

HS: You are only asked to give up all the nothing you never had. There is no "sacrifice" in giving up what causes you suffering. You demonstrate how tightly you grasp to fear by your extreme reactions to what you see. Forgive it all. Offer the world up to God as your single "sacrifice" to Him, in order that He may exchange it for what is real. Offer Him all your sadnesses, bitter disappointments, losses, grief and fear in exchange for His happiness. How do you make this transition? By stepping aside and allowing God to lead you. You must relinquish control over all outcomes. Merely follow, for you cannot lead.

324. I merely follow, for I would not lead.

HS: You cannot possibly lead, because your eyes are blind to the truth. You do not know the happy outcome of all things. However, I am within you, and I *do* know. God has set the way you should go and it is His plan you must follow. In this way, we walk together, as I guide you on your safe return Home. You are here to follow the path of forgiveness, in order that you may see a different world. All things you think you see reflect your ideas.

325. All things I think I see reflect ideas.

HS: When you are thinking with the ego, you see only as the ego sees. Do you want to continue to see pain and separation or Love and Unity? This is how your ability to create works. This is how you use your God given power. The problem is, your ego has thoughts of separation. The correction for these thoughts, is to remember that your One Life remains intact and undisturbed behind what you see now. You are the eternal and unchanging Loving Thought of God. He is the First Cause, and you are forever His Effect.

326. I am forever an Effect of God.

HS: You cannot change or destroy the Unchangeable. God is the Unmoved Mover. You hold these unchangeable attributes of God's Perfection within yourself, because He would not create a being lesser than Himself. All His power to create is yours, and you have made chaos. Now undo your mistake. Create on earth, as it is in Heaven. This is God's plan. Release the world to God's power to be transformed through calling on Him with forgiveness. He waits on you to call Him, and He will answer.

327. I need but call and You will answer me.

HS: You are not asked to accept salvation without proof that it is real. God has promised He will answer your call for help, but you do not know how to ask. You seem to have specific needs, stresses, and desires here in this world. You think you lack money, love, or some other amenity. You often pray for specific outcomes to singular problems. Salvation is the correction of *all* problems, which stem from just *one* problem; your imagined separation. It is *this* that you must call on God to help you with. You bear witness to His answer, as you experience your problems disappearing, one by one. Proof of His answer will be in the happier experience of your dream here, as it is gently transformed into one of joy, peace, and love. Step back, and allow God to direct your life. Choose the second place to gain the first.

328. I choose the second place to gain the first.

HS: The good news is, there *is* no second place. You are either joined with God's Will in first place, or not. There *is* nothing else. The world says that in order to gain freedom, one must separate off, "strike out on your own" and move away. The world says this is freedom. The Holy Spirit says that freedom is to rejoin with the whole, return to God, and share in His Power and Glory. Freedom is Oneness. To remember this, is salvation. You are saved from the loneliness, sickness, and death that await the traveler on the road of separation. Remember you are safe, whole, and eternally at peace in My Love. Happily give up your illusory journey of separation. This is God's Will for you, and you have already chosen what He Wills.

329. I have already chosen what You will.

HS: Because the separation never actually occurred, your Oneness with God remains unaltered. As it was in the beginning, is now, and ever shall be. You can cease to feel guilty. You have never defied your Holy Union with God, nor have you offended Him in any way. Why is it then, that you seem to continue to suffer here within the illusion? It is because you have not fully accepted your Union in truth. You still believe in the pain of separation. Choose to not hurt yourself.

330. I will not hurt myself again today.

HS: Whenever you feel even a small the twinge of pain, you should always respond with forgiveness. Forgiveness dissolves the ego and opens your mind; forgiveness says that pain is not real. With the ego set aside, your mind is now open and ready to receive miracles. All the miracle does, is show you that *you* are the dreamer of the dream. Through forgiveness, the miracle teaches you that all the power to change the dream has been placed within your own hands. You will then experience a shift in your dream of fear, to one of happiness, and your happy dream will then be transformed into the reality of Heaven. But first, you must cease to hurt yourself, by acknowledging you are not in conflict. It is God's Will that all conflict be healed within you, and your thoughts become peaceful.

. . .

ME: I am reminded here of a section of the TEXT that deals with something called, "The Happy Learner." Are we going to talk about this?

HS: Yes. In light of the recent problems you've been having keeping your mind at peace, I wanted to take a moment out of our discussions to help you become a more efficient learner. This will speed up the process of thought correction for you, and your life will begin to transform into a happier dream. We will begin discussing this topic here, and then finish in the next chapter.

ME: Well I suppose I could use all the help I can get. For some reason my thoughts sometimes go all over the place throughout the day; ranging up and down with corresponding emotions. Some days I feel serene and peaceful, while other days I'm, well, I'm the opposite of that. I can't seem to maintain my peace.

HS: This is because there are times when you are thinking with the ego, and times when you are choosing to think with Me. This creates inner turmoil and conflict. You cannot decide with whom you should be making decisions.

ME: Aren't my decisions my own? I mean, I feel pretty independent and that my mind is my own. I don't feel as though I'm consciously choosing to think with either the ego *or* You. I'm just having my own private thoughts and that's all.

HS: You cannot think alone. You do not exist independently, separate and apart, as you may feel. Your mind is connected to Me, and it is through the power of My Love that you exist. Without it, you would cease to be. However, when you deny connection to Me, you align your thoughts with the ego. The ego is *not a real entity*, but rather an *idea* you made up to mask your connection to Me. The ego is nothing. In other words, you are either thinking with Me, or you are thinking with nothing. When you join with nothing, you feel empty, isolated, and alone. There is no such thing as a private thought. You can only trick yourself into believing that it is possible.

ME: Hm. That's disconcerting. I don't like to think about the fact that there are no private thoughts. That feels so... Embarrassing!

HS: Only the ego is ever embarrassed by anything. Embarrassment is a form of shame, and shame is guilt, and the ego is born of guilt. You feel guilty at this moment in your learning, because you are aligned with your ego.

ME: Well, if I'm aligned with my ego right now, then how is it possible for me to hear *You?*

HS: You're only listening with the part of your mind that is still connected to Me. So you could say you're only *half* listening.

ME: How about we move on to that quote now?

The following quotations from the Course are from TEXT Chapter 14 — III. The Decision for Guiltlessness

"The happy learner cannot feel guilty about learning. This is so essential to learning that it should never be forgotten. The guiltless learner learns easily because his thoughts are free." (1:1-3)

"Perhaps you are accustomed to using guiltlessness merely to offset the pain of guilt, and do not look upon it as having value in itself." (2:1)

"There is no compromise that you can make with guilt, and escape the pain that only guiltlessness allays." (3:1)

Say therefore, to yourself, gently, but with the conviction born of the Love of God and of His Son:

What I experience I will make manifest.
If I am guiltless, I have nothing to fear.
I choose to testify to my acceptance of the Atonement, not to its rejection.
I would accept my guiltlessness by making it manifest and sharing it.
Let me bring peace to God's Son from his Father." (3:4-9)

"Each day, each hour and minute, even each second, you are deciding between the crucifixion and the resurrection;

between the ego and the Holy Spirit." (4:1)

"The miracle teaches you that you have chosen guiltlessness, freedom and joy." (5:1)

"No penalty is ever asked of God's Son except by himself and of himself." (6:1)

"The way to teach this simple lesson is merely this: Guiltlessness is invulnerability. Therefore, make your invulnerability manifest to everyone. Teach him that, whatever he may try to do to you, your perfect freedom from the belief that you can be harmed shows him that he is guiltless. He can do nothing that can hurt you, and by refusing to allow him to think he can, you teach him that the Atonement, which you have accepted for yourself, is also his. There is nothing to forgive. No one can hurt the Son of God. His guilt is wholly without cause, and being without cause, cannot exist." (7:1-7)

"Whenever you choose to make decisions for yourself you are thinking destructively, and the decision will be wrong." (9:1)

"Those who accept the Atonement *are* invulnerable." (10.:1)

"It will never happen that you must make decisions for yourself. You are not bereft of help, and Help that knows the answer." (11:1-2)

"Would you deny the truth of God's decision, and place your pitiful appraisal of yourself in place of His calm and unswerving value of His Son?" (12:1)

"Every decision you undertake alone but signifies that you would define what salvation *is*, and what you would be saved *from*. The Holy Spirit knows that all salvation is escape from guilt." (13:3-4)

"Let Him, therefore be the only Guide that you would follow to salvation. He knows the way, and leads you gladly on it." (14:1)

"Seek not to appraise the worth of God's Son whom He created holy, for to do so is to evaluate his Father and judge against Him." (15:1)

"Say to the Holy Spirit only, '"Decide for me,"' and it is done. For His decisions are reflections of what God knows about you, and in this light, error of any kind becomes impossible." (16:1-2)

"How gracious it is to decide all things through Him Whose equal Love is given equally to all alike!" (17:1)

"Whenever you are in doubt what you should do, think of His Presence in you, and tell yourself this, and only this:

He leadeth me and knows the way, which I know not.
Yet He will never keep from me what He would have me learn.
And so I trust Him to communicate to me all that He knows for me.

Then let Him teach you quietly how to perceive your guiltlessness, which is already there." (19:1-5)

ME: Sooooooo.... What does this all mean exactly?

HS: Depend on Me for your guidance instead of the ego. Do not react to anyone else as though the guilt they are trying to project onto you is real. Mind your business of forgiveness, and do not forget your shared innocence; no one can hurt or treat you unfairly, because you are all equally guiltless and invulnerable in truth.

ME: Jeez. What can't the Course just *say* that?

HS: If I simply gave you the answer to a complex math problem, would that answer have any meaning to you?

ME: You mean if You just said something like, "The answer is 42!" And I had no idea how You arrived at that answer?

HS: Yes.

ME: No, I guess not. I mean, I would have no appreciation for how that answer was arrived at. It'd just be a number like any other.

HS: Now what if I taught you how to work through the problem yourself; as painstaking, and difficult as it may seem at first; and then you arrived at the answer *yourself*? How would you feel about it then?

ME: Well, it would have much more meaning. It would represent all my efforts in learning, and I would be eager to teach others the steps it took to arrive at the correct answer too. I would want to help save them the time and struggle it took me to solve it.

HS: Precisely. And so it is with *A Course in Miracles*. It appears complicated, and its message hidden at first glance, simply because you do not understand the problem. But, as your learning progresses, and resistance from your ego lessens, its meaning gradually becomes clearer and clearer. I am trying to help you arrive at the answer yourself, so that it has greatest value to you, and then you may share it with others. If the Course were written any more simply, its message would be lost or overlooked entirely. You will find, that as your understanding of the Course increases, so will you begin to see its message written everywhere. Sayings you've read a thousand times will suddenly spring to life with new meaning. The problem has been, you've only seen the simple answer, and now you're being shown how to solve the complex problem behind it. Everything will look different from this new perspective as you apply My Answer to all you see.

ME: I *do* see. Learning *A Course in Miracles* is like learning a complex math problem; it teaches us how to solve our seeming problem of separation and arrive at the miraculous answer of our Oneness. I thought I understood that, but when You compare it to math, it makes even more sense. Except I'd say it's more like taking a course on Chinese algebra written in gibberish. Thank goodness I've got a Tutor.

HS: A good math teacher does not simply give his students the answer to the problem. They would learn nothing. Instead, he teaches them the method in solving the problem, and so the student owns the knowledge. I am here to teach you how to undo *all* your problems, by learning that your natural state, is a state of peace. There is no conflict, for My Will is peace, and you share My Will.

Chapter 27: Lessons 331-340

All We Want Is Peace

331. There is no conflict, for my will is Yours.

HS: As long as you see yourself as a body, you are in conflict between who you *think* you are, and Who You Are in truth. Except, there can be no conflict, because the ego is not real, and therefore there is nothing *to* conflict *with*. The conflict is of your own imagining. The world itself was born from the fear generated by this conflict, and it is fear that binds the world together. Forgiveness will set it free.

332. Fear binds the world. Forgiveness sets it free.

HS: All forms of fear that arise within you, bind yourself to this illusion. Choose to unchain it, and set yourself free through forgiveness. This is the miracle that comes from forgiveness. Forgiveness ends the dream of conflict here.

333. Forgiveness ends the dream of conflict here.

HS: There is no order of difficulty in correcting problems through forgiveness. Large or small, forgiveness corrects them all. God will not take the ego away from you against your will, but He will help you let go of it if you ask Him to. He has given you all the power in Heaven with which to do this, but you must claim the gifts forgiveness gives.

334. Today I claim the gifts forgiveness gives.

HS: God offers you His gift of Light in exchange for the shadows you made. Could anything less be good enough for God's Son? You have done nothing but make shadows. In forgiveness, you see past the shadow you cloaked your brother in, and know he has done nothing to you; he is sinless. It is God's Will that you choose to see your brother's sinlessness.

335. I choose to see my brother's sinlessness.

HS: Your body's eyes are incapable of showing you the truth. Because of this blindness, forgiveness must be something you *choose*. What you look like in reality, is far beyond what the body's eyes can show you. Therefore, you must choose to remember that you are Spirit, despite what your body's eyes show you. Through choosing to forgive, you see your One Self. Forgiveness lets you know that minds are joined.

336. Forgiveness lets me know that minds are joined.

HS: Forgiveness is the method with which you return to God. It is what you use to open your mind and allow Me to heal you. It is the technique required to know your Self. After forgiveness is complete, your perception of this world of illusions will end. What the change will look like, you cannot know, because it is beyond your comprehension while you still remain within the illusion. Trust in God's promises. All you need to do right now, is use the tool God has given you. Forgiveness turns your mind inward; the only place where the peace and safety of God can be found. Here is where you experience the safety of your joined Mind, your One sinless Self. Your sinlessness protects you from all harm.

337. My sinlessness protects me from all harm.

HS: You have taught yourselves that you are separated. What you teach, you learn. Now you must learn you are One Love. You must each accept this truth for yourselves in order to be healed of the separation. You are affected only by your own thoughts.

338. I am affected only by my thoughts.

HS: Once the power of your thoughts is realized with perfect honesty and clarity, you can use that power to heal the world. You have the power to choose to *change* what you think. Exchange your thoughts of fear for the one single Thought of Love: You are as God created you. You are One, and you are God's holy Son. You are not a body. Until this holy Thought of God is accepted, you will continue to crucify yourself; and you will receive whatever you request.

339. I will receive whatever I request.

HS: You are pursuing happiness in the wrong place. You are making the wrong request from the wrong source. You are asking for help from the ego, from which you will receive nothing, because the ego is nothing, and can give nothing. You must learn to make the correct request from the correct source; ask of God to rejoin with Love. Do this, and you can be free of suffering today.

340. I can be free of suffering today.

HS: You can be free of the ego now. Why not today? Why not this holy instant? You have come here for one reason and one reason only. You have come to end the dream of separation and awaken to Heaven in the Heart of Love.

. . .

ME: I want to forgive the world, I truly do! I want to "awaken to Heaven in the Heart of Love." Now why isn't it happening for me? This is so frustrating.

HS: You came across a quote this morning dealing with your function in the Atonement. Please insert that here.

The following quotations from the Course are from TEXT Chapter 14 — IV. Your Function in the Atonement

"Ask not to be forgiven, for this has already been accomplished. Ask, rather, to learn how to forgive, and to restore what always was to your unforgiving mind. Atonement becomes real and visible to those who use it. On earth this is your only function, and you must learn that it is all you want to learn." (3:3-7)

"God breaks no barriers; neither did He make them. When you release them they are gone." (4:2-3)

HS: This is saying that what your forgiveness accomplishes, *will* manifest visibly in your life. But you must have patience. For most, awakening to the Atonement is a gradual process; it doesn't happen overnight, although there may be sudden leaps forward that may surprise you. The barriers you have made between God and yourself come down through one forgiveness at a time. He would not further frighten you by awakening you too suddenly.

ME: I see. But what about the holy instant? Doesn't that happen- in an instant?

HS: When a child has a nightmare, a good parent sits beside the child and gently caresses them, speaking soft words of comfort until they awaken of their own will. The parent does not shake them; that would only further disorient the child and frighten them, causing an even greater delay in their full awakening. So it is between Myself and all My sleeping children. I see that you dream terrible things, yet I sit beside you, gently loving you, calling you to awaken. If I moved in too quickly, before you were ready, it would do more harm than good. And so I patiently wait until each child opens its eyes on its own, ready for My Light. Once your eyes open, all darkness will vanish- in a holy instant.

ME: Oh, so until then, we seem to suffer in our nightmare, but we're actually slowly moving through an awakening process? Even if the dream seems as far from awakening as it could possibly get?

HS: Correct. However, life will get much easier for you as you align your thoughts with Mine. You will see your struggles greatly diminish, although in the beginning your life may appear to be falling apart. Rejoice! This is all part of the undoing process, which leads to your awakening. All that is happening, is that whatever is keeping you asleep is being removed from your life. It may appear as loss at first; but I tell you, these losses are your greatest gains. Loss creates space in your life for miracles.

The following quotation from the Course is from
TEXT Chapter 21 — I. The Forgotten Song

"There is no need to learn through pain. And gentle lessons are acquired joyously, and are remembered gladly." (3:1-2)

**The following quotations from the Course are from
TEXT Chapter 21 — II. The Responsibility for Sight**

"This is the only thing that you need do for vision, happiness, release from pain and the complete escape from sin, all to be given you. Say only this, but mean it with no reservations, for here the power of salvation lies:

*I **am** responsible for what I see.*
I choose the feelings I experience, and I decide
upon the goal I would achieve.
And everything that seems to happen to me
I ask for, and receive as I have asked.

Deceive yourself no longer that you are helpless in the face of what is done to you. Acknowledge but that you have been mistaken, and all effects of your mistakes will disappear." (2:1-7)

"No accident or chance is possible within the universe as God created it, outside of which is nothing." (3:4)

"Be happy, and you gave the power of decision to Him Who must decide for God for you. This is the little gift you offer to the Holy Spirit, and even this He gives to you to give yourself." (3:6-7)

ME: I have trouble aligning my thoughts with Yours. I feel like they just wander all over the place and I can't stop them.

HS: Stopping them is not the issue. The issue is simply recognizing which ones are real, and which ones are false.

**The following quotations from the Course are from
TEXT Chapter 14 — X. The Equality of Miracles**

"Perhaps you have been aware of lack of competition among your thoughts, which even though they may conflict, can occur together and in great numbers. You may indeed be so used to this that it causes you little surprise." (4:1-2)

"For some are reflections of Heaven, while others are motivated by the ego, which but seems to think." (4:5)

"The result is a weaving, changing pattern that never rests and is never still. It shifts unceasingly across the mirror of your mind, and the reflections of Heaven last but a moment and grow dim, as darkness blots them out." (5:1-2)

"It will seem difficult for you to learn that you have no basis at all for ordering your thoughts. This lesson the Holy Spirit teaches by giving you the shining examples of miracles to show you that your way of ordering is wrong, but that a better way is offered you." (6:1-2)

"The only judgement involved is the Holy Spirit's one division into two categories; one of love, and the other the call for love. You cannot safely make this division, for you are much too confused either to recognize love, or to believe that everything else is nothing but a call for love." (7:1-2)

"It is impossible to remember God in secret and alone. For remembering Him means you are not alone, and are willing to remember it." (10:1-2)

"The miracle is the recognition that this is true. Where there is love, your brother must give it to you because of what it is. But where there is a call for love, you must give it because of what you are. Earlier I said this course will teach you how to remember what you are, restoring to you your Identity. We have already learned that this Identity is shared. The miracle becomes the means of sharing It." (12:1-6)

ME: So what should I do about my scattered thoughts?

HS: Allow the loving ones, and *give* love to the unloving ones.

ME: Oh. That's not too complicated.

HS: Indeed, to the practiced forgiver, it is simple. But in your case, I will go over further guidelines to get you through those times you find yourself "in the heat of the moment," as you so described earlier. Now we will continue on with the second part of our discussion from the previous chapter. Here then are the rules for decision making; rules to guide you in organizing your thoughts to ensure you are always thinking with Me, and not the ego.

The following quotations from the Course are from TEXT Chapter 30 — I. Rules for Decision

"Decisions are continuous. You do not always know when you are making them. But with a little practice with the ones you recognize, a set begins to form which sees you through the rest." (1:1-3)

"The proper set, adopted consciously each time you wake, will put you well ahead." (1:5)

"But think about the kind of day you want, and tell yourself there is a way in which this very day can happen just like that." (1:8)

"The outlook starts with this:

Today I will make no decisions by myself.

This means that you are choosing not to be the judge of what to do." (2:1-3)

"Throughout the day, at any time you think of it and have a quiet moment for reflection, tell yourself again the kind of day you want; the feelings you would have, the things you want to happen to you, and the things you would experience, and say:

If I make no decisions by myself, this is the day that will be given me." (4:1-2)

"But there will still be times when you have judged already. (5:1)

This means you have decided by yourself, and can not see the question. Now you need a quick restorative before you ask again." (5:4-5)

"Then realize that you have asked a question by yourself, and must have set an answer in your terms. Then say:

I have no question. I forgot what to decide." (6:2-4)

"Try to observe this rule without delay, despite your opposition. For you have already gotten angry." (7:1-2)

"If you are so unwilling to receive you cannot even let your question go, you can begin to change your mind with this:

At least I can decide I do not like what I feel now. (8:1-2)

"Having decided that you do not like the way you feel, what could be easier than to continue with:

And so I hope I have been wrong." (9:1-2)

"Now you have reached the turning point, because it has occurred to you that you will gain if what you have decided is not so." (10:1)

"And you can say in perfect honesty:

I want another way to look at this." (11:3-4)

"This final step is but acknowledgment of lack of opposition to be helped. It is a statement of an open mind, not certain yet, but willing to be shown:

Perhaps there is another way to look at this.

What can I lose by asking?" (12:1-4)

"It must be clear that it is easier to have a happy day if you prevent unhappiness from entering at all. But this takes practice in the rules that will protect you from the ravages of fear." (13:1-2)

"Your day is not at random. It is set by what you choose to live it with, and how the friend whose counsel you have sought perceives your happiness." (15:1-2)

"Decisions cause results because they are not made in isolation. They are made by you and your adviser, for yourself and for the world as well. (16:5-6) What kind of day will you decide to have?" (16:9)

"It needs but two. These two are joined before there can be a decision. Let this be the one reminder that you keep in mind, and you will have the day you want, and give it to the world by having it yourself. Your judgment has been lifted from the world by your decision for a happy day. And as you have received, so must you give." (17:4-8)

ME: Okay, so can You just sum this up for me, as You always do?

HS: Always decide you want My peace instead of conflict and you will be happy.

ME: That's it?

HS: That's it.

ME: Hm. Well that sounds simple enough.

HS: It *is* simple, but first you must choose My peace, and then accept it. This is the rule for making a decision about what kind of day you want. You always want a peaceful, happy day, and that can only be attained by remembering to decide for this with Me. It needs but two; you and I, or you and the ego- and the ego is nothing, so it is a decision made by yourself alone.

ME: Ah there's the catch. *Remembering* to choose Your peace and assistance. Sometimes it's hard for me to do that. I feel like I have attention deficit disorder or something when it comes to remembering I want Your peace.

HS: Don't worry. Pain and all forms and levels of discomfort will rush in to remind you when you've forgotten. When you find yourself lost at sea in a storm, remember all you want is My peace. This will bring your thoughts into alignment with Mine, and a happy day will arise before your eyes. And it's never too late to start your day over. You can remember you want My peace even as you lie in bed preparing for sleep. Each night, give yourself this gift: that you cease to attack yourself and know it is My peace that keeps you safe. You are sinless.

Chapter 28: Lessons 341-350

This World Is A School

341. I can attack but my own sinlessness,
And it is only that which keeps me safe.

HS: What is sinlessness but a state of Perfect Love and Union? When you attack one another, you attack your Union, and therefore your sinlessness. Only through your Perfect Union are you safe. Do not try to destroy the only thing that keeps you safe. Therefore, let your forgiveness rest upon all things, for thus is forgiveness given you.

342. I let forgiveness rest upon all things,
For thus forgiveness will be given me.

HS: Forgiveness cannot be forced upon the world; it is allowed to *rest* on all things by you. Use forgiveness to lift your judgments from the world and forgiveness will be given you in return. You are included in your own forgiveness. Forgiveness asks for no sacrifice form you, but asks instead that you simply replace your idea of separation, with the mercy and peace of God.

343. I am not asked to make a sacrifice
To find the mercy and the peace of God.

HS: You are asked to sacrifice nothing, in exchange for everything. And the world *is* indeed nothing. Give up guilt and damnation, and you free each other through the gift of forgiveness. You must learn the law of love; that what you give your brother, is your gift to yourself.

344. Today I learn the law of love; that what
I give my brother is my gift to me.

HS: God's Love is all-inclusive. It is Oneness. If this is truth, then to love another, is to love yourself. The world teaches that some of you can be excluded from love or loved less than another. The world teaches that love is something that can be taken away, lost, or withheld. The Holy Spirit teaches that you each contain the same Love, in equal amount. The miracle undoes

216

the error of your loveless perception of one another. Offer only miracles to one another, for you would have them be returned to you.

345. I offer only miracles today, For I would have them be returned to me.

HS: Life as you experience it now, is a direct reflection of what you have offered yourself. You receive according to the tenor of our thoughts, which contain all the power of God. If you do not like what you experience within this dream, then you must change what you think. How long will you continue to crucify yourself? All your thoughts are reflected back to you in some form. Therefore, let the peace of God envelope you, and forget all things except His Love.

346. Today the peace of God envelops me, And I forget all things except His Love.

HS: You are not being asked here to accept or condemn another's behaviors. Rather, you are being asked to admit you do not understand the purpose of anything. Forgiveness asks you to look upon all things, people, and yourself as though you see them for the first time; in innocence, without attack, and without fear. In this way, you give your mind over to God, wiped clean of all anger and judgment. Anger comes from judgment, and it is the weapon you would use against yourself, to keep miracles away from you.

347. Anger must come from judgment. Judgment is The weapon I would use against myself, To keep the miracle away from me.

HS: Anger is a sure sign you have separated from God's Will. It is a sure sign you are following your ego. Anger is the means with which you force your judgment upon a situation you know nothing about in truth. Anger is a miracle delaying device. You have no cause for anger of fear. God surrounds you. And in every need that you perceive, His grace suffices you.

348. I have no cause for anger or for fear, For You surround me. And in every need That I perceive, Your grace suffices me.

HS: Why rage against a dream? Your effort is wasted on it. Leave it alone. By not reacting to it as real, you take away its power. The ego does not want you to think you may have been wrong, that there is something else to see; something better. Faith in God's grace is all you need to surmount all temptations you see here. Allow Christ's vision to look upon all things for you, and judge them not. Give each one a miracle of love instead.

349. Today I let Christ's vision look upon All things for me and judge them not, but give Each one a miracle of love instead.

HS: Forgiveness says, "I am not fooled by what I see. I know I am seeing the world and all the people in it, incorrectly. We are not bodies. I know we are God's One Son." Each forgiveness you extend to the world in this way, is a miracle. These miracles mirror God's eternal Love. To offer them is to remember Him, and through His memory you save the world.

350. Miracles mirror God's eternal Love. To offer them is to remember Him, And through His memory to save the world.

HS: It is a miracle to remember that there is another world beyond this one that you desire. A world that your Father Created with Love. As you remember God's Presence in all living things, the memory of your Sonship and freedom in Him will be restored to you. You must decide to see one another as sinless Spirit, instead of a sinful body. One way of seeing will bring you peace and the other pain. And which you choose to see, is the reality you will behold.

. . .

ME: You've spent a lot of time teaching me about how I'm seeing the world wrongly and how to correct it, but You haven't really explained the benefits clearly. I would like to hear more about the positive changes forgiveness promises. I want to hear more about Your plan for us.

HS: I would gladly share more about My plan with you. Let's begin with a quote.

ME: Sigh. Of course. Another quote. Can't You just tell me *without* a quote for once?

HS: This is all part of My teaching plan for you.

The following quotation from the Course is from TEXT Chapter 20 — IV. Entering the Ark

"You may wonder how you can be at peace when, while you are in time, there is so much that must be done before the way to peace is open. Perhaps this seems impossible to you. But ask yourself if it is possible that God would have a plan for your salvation that does not work. Once you accept His plan as the one function that you would fulfill, there will be nothing else the Holy Spirit will not arrange for you without your effort. He will go before you making straight your path, and leaving in your way no stones to trip on, and no obstacles to bar your way. Nothing you need will be denied you. Not one seeming difficulty but will melt away before you reach it. You need take thought for nothing, carless of everything except the only purpose that you would fulfill. As that was given you, so will its fulfillment be. God's guarantee will hold against all obstacles, for it rests on certainty and not on contingency. It rests on *you*. And what can be more certain than a Son of God?" (8:1-12)

ME: So basically, as we become better "forgivers" our path through this world becomes easier?

HS: Yes.

ME: So what should I think when things go wrong or become difficult? For instance, just this morning I injured my lower back while lifting a few horse feed bags. The pain literally drove me to my knees. Right now, I am lying on my stomach in the middle of the living room floor as I type this, because it's too painful to sit upright. Is this injury a sign I'm backsliding or somehow doing poorly with my forgiveness lessons?

HS: Absolutely not. When you experience trying times, whether it be emotional or physical; always take it as a sign that positive spiritual change is upon you. Your body and your life situations will always seem to "act up" or get worse as you stand upon the cusp of a great spiritual leap forward. Your ego will often attempt to reestablish that it is real by attempting to increase pain or drama in your life. Forgive it all and rejoice in your struggles! They are but the harbingers of good things to come for you.

ME: Okay, I'll try to forgive my ego for attempting to convince me that my body is real through this horrible back pain. This is tough though. Are You sure I haven't done something wrong to manifest this?

HS: You have done nothing wrong. Once you know that all your pain and suffering stems from your own thoughts, it is tempting to then feel guilty about that; as though you have done something "wrong" to deserve it. *This is not so!* These are but forgiveness lessons being presented to you, and nothing more.

ME: Well I guess the sooner I forgive the world, the better then. I want to be done with this pain!

HS: I wish to make it very clear that you should not look upon the world as your enemy. Unfortunate circumstances are all part of My divine plan, and I am here to work *with* you, not *against* you. Always use common sense, forethought, and planning when it comes to your life, but do not worry about any of it once you have done so. It is all part of My plan for your happy release. The only thing My plan requires, is that you need do nothing.

The following quotations from the Course are from TEXT Chapter 18 — VII. I Need Do Nothing

"You still have too much faith in the body as a source of strength. What plans do you make that do not involve its comfort or protection or enjoyment in some way?" (1:1-2)

"There is one thing that you have never done; you have not utterly forgotten the body." (2:1)

"At no single instant does the body exist at all. It is always remembered or anticipated, but never experienced just *now*. Only its past and future make it seem real." (3:1-3)

"It is impossible to accept the holy instant without reservation unless, just for an instant, you are willing to see no past or future." (4:1)

"Many have spent a lifetime in preparation, and have indeed achieved their instants of success. This course does not attempt to teach more than they learned in time, but it does aim at saving time." (4:4-5)

"Your way will be different, not in purpose but in means. A holy relationship is a means of saving time. One instant spent together with your brother restores the universe to both of you. You *are* prepared. Now you need but to remember you need do nothing." (5:1-5)

"I need do nothing" is a statement of allegiance, a truly undivided loyalty. Believe it for one instant, and you will accomplish more than is given to a century of contemplation, or of struggle against temptation." (6:7-8)

"To do anything involves the body. And if you recognize you need do nothing, you have withdrawn the body's value from your mind." (7:1-2)

"This quiet center, in which you do nothing, will remain with you, giving you rest in the midst of every busy doing on which you are sent." (8:3)

ME: So You're essentially saying here that we worry too much, is that it?

HS: Yes. There is nothing in the illusion you should ever worry about. This world is nothing more than a school and the lesson you are here to learn is that you need do nothing to return to Me. You already have Me.

ME: Hm. I feel I'm already pretty good at "doing nothing," but it doesn't seem to have awakened me to Your Presence. How much more "nothing" do I need to do?

HS: To "do nothing" is to give the dream you are a body over to Me, and I will use it to teach you of your true Identity. Right now, you are most certainly doing *something;* you are believing in separation. Give your bodily eyes and ears over to Me, and I will show you the holiness that lies beyond what these feeble senses show you. The body is the only limit you have placed upon yourself for knowing Me.

The following quotations from the Course are from TEXT Chapter 18 — VIII. The Little Garden

"It is only the awareness of the body that makes love seem limited. For the body *is* a limit on love." (1:1-2)

"You cannot even think of God without a body, or in some form you think you recognize." (1:7)

"The body cannot know. And while you limit your awareness to its tiny senses, you will not see the grandeur that surrounds you." (2:1-2)

"Within this kingdom the ego rules, and cruelly. And to defend this little speck of dust it bids you fight against the universe." (3:1-2)

"The body is a tiny fence around a little part of a glorious and complete idea." (3:5)

"Such is the strange position in which those in a world inhabited by bodies seem to be. Each body seems to house a separate mind, a disconnected thought, living alone and in no way joined to the Thought by which it was created." (5:1-2)

"This little self is not your kingdom. Arched high above it and surrounding it with love is the glorious whole, which offers all its happiness and deep content to every part." (7:6-7)

"The Thought of God surrounds your little kingdom, waiting at the barrier you built to come inside and shine upon the barren ground." (9:1)

"The holy instant is your invitation to love to enter into your bleak and joyless kingdom, and to transform it into a garden of peace and welcome." (11:1)

ME: So the holy instant, is the moment I finally move past what I believe the body's senses are showing me. The moment I let all my barriers to Your love fall?

HS: Yes. The holy instant is the instant you understand that you understand nothing as it is in truth. You remove your judgment from the world and what you think it is and what it is for. The holy instant is the moment you let go of all the fear you think surrounds you; knowing it is a false reality.

The following quotations from the Course are from
TEXT Chapter 18 — IX. The Two Worlds

"Be you not separate, for the One Who does surround it has brought Union to you, returning your little offering of darkness to the eternal light. How is this done? It is extremely simple, being based on what this little kingdom really is." (2:1-3)

"From the world of bodies, made by insanity, insane messages seem to be retuned to the mind that made it. And these messages bear witness to this world, pronouncing it as true." (3:1-2)

"There are no messages that speak of what lies underneath, for it is not the body that could speak of this." (3:5)

"Yet God can bring you there, if you are willing to follow the Holy Spirit through seeming terror, trusting Him not to abandon you and leave you there." (3:7)

"The circle of fear lies just below the level the body sees, and seems to be the whole foundation on which the world is based. Here are all the illusions, all the twisted thoughts, all the insane attacks, the fury, the vengeance and betrayal that were made to keep the guilt in place, so that the world could rise from it and keep it hidden." (4:1-2)

"The body cannot see this, for the body arose from this for its protection, which depends on keeping it not seen. The body's eyes will never look on it. Yet they will see what it dictates." (4:5-7)

"This heavy-seeming barrier, this artificial floor that looks like rock, is like a bank of low dark clouds that seem to be a solid wall before the sun." (6:1)

"You will not bruise yourself against them in traveling through. Let your Guide teach you their unsubstantial nature as He leads you past them, for beneath them is a world of light where on they cast no shadows." (8;2-3)

"This world of light, this circle of brightness is the real world, where guilt meets with forgiveness." (9:1)

"Forgiveness does make lovely, but it does not create. It is the source of healing, but it is the messenger of love and not its Source." (10:1-2)

"A step beyond this holy place of forgiveness, a step still further inward but the one *you* cannot take, transports you to something completely different." (10:5)

"Forgiveness removes the untrue, lifting the shadows from the world and carrying it, safe and sure within its gentleness, to the bright world of new and clean perception. There is your purpose *now*. And it is there that peace awaits you." (14:3-4)

ME: So You say this world is actually like a school to be used for teaching us forgiveness of the illusion; for correcting our error in thinking we know what is real.

HS: Yes.

ME: This reminds me of yet another dream I had about this world being a school.

HS: Do share it now please.

ME: I dreamt I was standing outside a dreary looking school, wondering how to enter and help the students trapped inside. They didn't seem to know that while they were inside a building with blackened windows, a wonderful world of light lay just outside. The school taught them that the world of light didn't exist, and that the small pain-filled world they sat in was their only reality. All they had to do was look up from the toil and suffering they were studying at their desks and accept for just an instant, that there might be something else. Something better. I was anxious to help them, so I went around the school looking for windows that were open even just a crack, tossing in crunched up paper balls with the message of light written on them. I also placed messages at all the doors, just in case anyone decided to open them in an attempt to come outside. I wanted to make sure everyone knew they had a choice to come into the Light, because I loved them.

HS: Yes, that is how this illusion is for you all here.

ME: So here I am, sitting at my "desk" in this world, experiencing pain. Now I need to "look up," and switch teachers? Or look for a "note" someone threw in through the "window?"

HS: Yes, and you've already found a good note. You've found *A Course in Miracles.*

ME: Oh! I love that thought.

HS: The message of Light is written in many other places as well. It comes in many ways, and many forms, but the message will always be the saME: Your sinless brother is your guide to peace. Your sinful brother is your guide to pain. And which you choose to see, is the world you will behold.

Chapter 29: Lessons 351-360

When Everything Seems To Fall Apart

351. My sinless brother is my guide to peace.
My sinful brother is my guide to pain.
And which I choose to see I will behold.

HS: If you choose to see one another as bodies (sinful), then you are choosing the ego as your guide. If you choose to see My Light (sinlessness) within others, you are choosing Me as your Guide to peace. Because you are imperfect judges, ask Me to be the judge of what you see. I alone can be the judge, because only I alone know All. From your judgment come all the sorrows of the world, and from My Love comes the peace of God Himself.

352. Judgment and love are opposites. From one
Come all the sorrows of the world. But from
The other comes the peace of God Himself.

HS: Through judgment you see separation, and through love you see Unity. Judgment is un-forgiveness, while Love is total forgiveness. Let your mind be still, as you give yourself over to Me through forgiveness of what you see. This allows My Voice to speak to you. Your eyes, your tongue, your hands, your feet have but one purpose; to be given Christ to use to bless the world with miracles.

353. My eyes, my tongue, my hands, my feet today
Have but one purpose; to be given Christ
To use to bless the world with miracles.

HS: Your bodily senses work perfectly. They show you 100% error everywhere, and this is what they are designed to do. You need not feel guilty about this, as you have done nothing wrong, and God is not angry with you for it. He would merely free you from it. And so, you must give all that you have over to Him to use in the purpose you share with Him. You must make a different choice; to repurpose your body for forgiveness. In so doing, you bless the world with miracles. Through recognition of your errors, you work alongside God to serve your appointed function here. You stand together with Christ in peace and certainty of purpose. And in Him is His Creator, as He is in you.

354. We stand together, Christ and I in peace And certainty of purpose. And in Him Is His Creator, as He is in me.

HS: You have no other purpose here, but to learn the truth of Who You Are. God Created Christ exactly like Himself, and what are you except part of Christ? Through Him you work miracles. Not of your own power, but of His. Once you accept God's Word that you are part of His holy Sonship, there is no end to all the peace and joy, and all the miracles that you will give. Why not accept His Word today?

355. There is no end to all the peace and joy, And all the miracles that I will give, When I accept God's Word. Why not today?

HS: You have traveled to this dream and are seemingly far and distant from your Home. You feel exiled from Heaven. Yet God has promised you that you will *all* return to Him. What are you waiting for? Why not accept you are His Son? You have endless miracles within your grasp and yet you sit in suffering and loneliness. All you need do, is make a choice. A simple choice between two identities: the Son of God or the ego. You now know that either loving gifts or suffering go along with each choice. Choose to heal sin and sickness through forgiveness. Sickness is simply another name for sin, and healing is another name for God. The miracle then, is a call to Him.

356. Sickness is but another name for sin. Healing is but another name for God. The miracle is thus a call to Him.

HS: Your mind is sick indeed in that you cannot remember your oneness in God. Your mind is divided between God and the ego. To heal this split, you must call for healing through forgiving thoughts. Forgiveness is the maximal expression of love that you can give. Forgiveness says that you choose not to put your faith in what you see, but only in the Love *within* your brother. And so, *when you forgive, you call to God using His own Voice, through His Own Word, and in His Own Name.* You invoke the power of His Love when you forgive. His Love is then reflected back to you. Truth will always answer every call you make to God, responding first with miracles, and then returning to you to be itself.

357. Truth answers every call we make to God, Responding first with miracles, and then Returning unto us to be itself.

HS: Love will always respond to the call of Love. It knows Its Own Voice. You speak the language of Love when you forgive. This is because forgiveness reflects the truth of how things really are. Once you accept that you have fabricated a world in error, *you know exactly how to offer miracles.* And what you give, you will receive. Forgiveness calls out to Me within your brothers first, and then you will know Me within yourself. No call to God can be unheard nor left unanswered. And of this you can be sure; His answer is the only one you really want.

358. No call to God can be unheard nor left Unanswered. And of this I can be sure; His answer is one I really want.

HS: Here is where faith and trust develop to superhuman levels. Only God remembers Who You Are and because of this, you must allow only Me to speak on your behalf. Remember that you are completely blind here within the illusion and you cannot see yourself or anyone else as they truly are. Let the voice of your ego be still, while you listen only to Me, Whose Voice unceasingly proclaims: Your One Self is *all there is, and you are at peace.* This will always be God's answer to every problem you think you have. His answer will always be some form of peace. All your pain and misery will be replaced with joy. All prison doors will open as all sin is understood as merely a mistake.

359. God's answer is some form of peace. All pain Is healed; all misery replaced with joy.

All prison doors are opened. And all sin
Is understood as merely a mistake.

HS: Who You Truly Are, remains safe and untouched by what you see and experience within this world. You have misunderstood all things. In deepest forgiveness of your own errors, step back and let Creation be as God Created it. And so rejoice, knowing that the illusion you made has no effect on you at all. In this understanding, you will find peace. Peace be to you, the holy Son of God. Peace to your brothers, who are one with you. Let all the world be blessed with peace through you.

360. Peace be to me, the holy Son of God.
Peace be to my brother, who is one with me.
Let all the world be blessed with peace through us.

HS: What is peace, but to be without conflict?   Lay down the heavy emotional burdens of the world with a huge sigh of relief. To give up conflict is to humbly accept that you do not know anything as it truly is. There is nothing to judge, because you do not know what you are looking at. To admit that you have been wrong about everything, allows a deep silence to come over your mind, as you relinquish all your thoughts to Me. This opens the door to truth. You have done nothing but dream a dream. You are all innocent. You remain perfect as you were created, no matter how hard you've tried to imagine yourself otherwise. Be thankful nothing you dreamed was true. The world is forgiven. You will remain forever and always, God's holy Son. And to this We say "Amen."

. . .

ME: What You say here is all very nice. It truly is. I'm glad that You can see us As We Truly Are, and I'm glad that You're happy and content; continuously existing as One Love. I really am. That's all very nice for You. However, I've had a rather rough week down here in this illusion of time and space, and I still don't understand how this all fits in with Your plan for my happiness.

HS: I would love nothing more than to help you understand. Please go on.

ME: I understand that I see nothing as it is in truth. I get it, that I'm blind with these bodily eyes. I truly believe that once I begin to use my inner eyes to see, and forgive my outer world, that things will improve. I have faith in Your promise that life will get easier and better. However, right now my life seems to be totally falling apart. I know You said it might do that, but hear me out.

HS: I'm listening.

ME: Okay. So this past weekend, my daughter's beloved hamster died. (And I mean she truly *loved* him. She took him with her everywhere she could). We all shed a few tears, but he was old, and it was expected. It was sad, but fine. Next I discovered one of my horses had an infection in her rear leg that swelled up to the size of a football and she needed emergency treatment. Alright, I can cope with that. *Then* I threw my back out moving a few 50-pound bags of horse feed, which currently has me in a near constant state of pain. Not great, but I can accept this too. And last but not least, I administered a flu shot at my pharmacy to my dad, *and I nearly killed him!* He had a reaction to it and ended up in the emergency room. *Seriously?!* I mean, of the all people to end up in the hospital from a flu shot I administered, it had to be my *dad?* I've given thousands of flu shots over the past five years, and no one has *ever* had a reaction! But the first person to have one, just so happens to be my *dad?* All of this took place over a two-day span.

HS: I believe there's more. Please continue.

ME: You bet there is. So three days after all this, I had what I call my "bad mail day." Everything in the mail was bad. First, we received a bill from our daughter's gymnastics school for three hundred and seventy five dollars for lessons we never signed her up for. Then I opened a letter from the Board of Pharmacy, stating that I was randomly selected for an audit of my continuing education credits this year. Next I opened an email from our daughter's piano teacher, stating she still hadn't received last month's payment. Apparently it had been lost. Last but not least, we received another email from our credit card agency, stating that our credit card was being used out of state, and fraudulent charges had accrued to upwards of two thousand dollars!!! All of this happened *on one day!* What gives? Enough is enough already! When will all this stop? I'm ready for the "happy dream" any time.

HS: My dear child. I will explain this to you in as many different ways as it takes, until you understand.

ME: Please do. Just one more time. I promise I'll pay close attention.

HS: I do not promise to deliver you from all your adversities and trials, but I *do* promise to go with you through all of them. Trust Me. You don't want the seemingly "good" parts of your dream either. All parts of the dream equally hold you back and keep you from your peace. Quote please.

The following quotations from the Course are from TEXT Chapter 29 — IV. Dream Roles

"The dreams you think you like would hold you back as much as those in which the fear is seen. For every dream is but a dream of fear, no matter what the form it seems to take. The fear is seen within, without, or both. Or it can be disguised in pleasant form. But never is it absent from the dream, for fear is the material of dreams, from which they all are made. Their form can change, but they cannot be made of something else." (2:1-6)

"Depression or assault must be the theme of every dream, for they are made of fear. The thin disguise of pleasure and of joy in which they may be wrapped but slightly veils the heavy lump of fear that is their core. And it is this the miracle perceives, and not the wrappings in which it is bound." (3:3-5)

"When you are angry, is it not because someone has failed to fill the function you allotted him? And does this not become the "reason" your attack is justified? The dreams you think you like are those in which the functions you have given have

231

been filled; the needs which you ascribe to you are met. It does not matter if they be fulfilled or merely wanted. It is the idea that they exist from which the fears arise." (4:1-5)

"How happy would your dreams become if you were not the one who gave the "proper" role to every figure which the dream contains." (5:1)

ME: I see. So because I have certain *expectations* about how things should go or how people should act, that causes my unhappiness?

HS: Correct. The very fact that you think your happiness depends on another's behavior, health, or words, is what seems to bring you "bad experiences." People almost *never* do what you want. Things may seem to go your way at times, but only because the people you have given roles to, are playing them as you'd like. Their body is still alive, or they haven't left you, or no one is stealing from you, or they are behaving in some way that pleases you. Yet, it is still all part of the dream, and dreams do not last. Let go of your assigned roles to the figures in your dream; including yourself.

ME: But You've said that it's okay for me to enjoy the good times, right? I shouldn't feel guilty about that?

HS: Yes, but know that the things you love most about the illusion can actually be the most difficult to lay down. It is equally true that through your greatest trials that you make your greatest gains. You are each like an unlit match. When the proper amount of friction and pressure is applied, you ignite into a blazing light of glory. And once lit, your flame will be transferred to as many as are willing to accept it.

ME: I think I have a wet match. I don't really like "friction and pressure."

HS: Do not seek to escape every hardship. Seek rather, to be the example of how to bear your burdens with dignity, grace, and love. Accept *what is*. This is what it means to live in a state of grace. To live in a state of grace, means to continue to love in a loveless world. It is a state in which you step back from all the drama, all the hate, and all the fear, and just simply *be*. You dwell with Me, on a path of love, far above the battleground, peacefully allowing the pain of this world to pass you by. Let it go in peace. And so your path becomes easy, your burdens will lift before your very eyes, and you will move ahead with the speed of My Light. You will come to relish your challenges as you learn how quickly they ascend you to new spiritual heights. Strive to become a champion of misfortune and disappointment. Then you will experience the "happy dream" you are looking for.

ME: Well is it alright to pray to You for help with painful things, and to keep people safe and healthy? I just don't enjoy suffering and loss I guess.

HS: Always pray first for yourself that you may see things correctly. Pray to let go of all outcomes, and give them to Me. Your only job is to accept *what is*. Do not pray for specific outcomes as you see them. You will be wrong every time. Would you rather be forcefully driven forward by the ego, or lead gently and peacefully ahead by Me? The choice is always yours.

ME: I think I finally get it. Thank Heavens. Thank *You*.

HS: Remember: forgiveness does not automatically make everything *okay*, but it *does* automatically make *you* okay with *everything*. It is through the simple practice of forgiveness that you will surmount all your difficulties and resurrect to Me at last. Change your mind about what this world is for and your place in it. Accept your Oneness in My Spirit. Only this is real. Only this is truth.

The following quotations from the Course are from MANUAL FOR TEACHERS
28. What Is the Resurrection?

"Very simply, the resurrection is the overcoming or surmounting of death. It is a reawakening or a rebirth; a change of mind about the meaning of the world. It is the acceptance of the Holy Spirit's interpretation of the world's purpose; the acceptance of the Atonement for oneself. It is the end of dreams of misery, and the glad awareness of the

Holy Spirit's final dream. It is the recognition of the gifts of God. It is the dream in which the body functions perfectly, having no function except communication. It is the lesson in which learning ends, for it is consummated and surpassed with this. It is the invitation to God to take His final step. It is the relinquishment of all other purposes, all other interests, all other wishes and all other concerns. It is the single desire of the Son for the Father." (1:1-10)

"Here the curriculum ends." (3:1)

"No hidden places now remain on earth to shelter sick illusions, dreams of fear and misperceptions of the universe. All things are seen in light, and in the light their purpose is transformed and understood. And we, God's children, rise up from the dust and look upon our perfect sinlessness. The song of Heaven sounds around the world, as it is lifted up and brought to truth." (4:5-8)

ME: This reminds me of yet another dream You sent me. The final dream out of a total of thirteen I received while studying these Workbook lessons; dreams that came once every tenth night beginning with lesson 221. The one I am thinking of is titled "The Tree of Life." I dreamt that You sent me to a faraway land to plant three seeds. When I arrived at the faraway land, I saw that it was covered in nothing but dry, dead grass. The ground was hard and full of deep cracks. So I walked on for a while, searching for a suitable place to plant the seeds You'd put me in charge of. Eventually I came to a small patch of fertile ground, and kneeling before this, I plunged the seeds deep into the soil. Then I stepped back and watched as a magnificent tree grew from these seeds. It was The Tree of Life, through which we could all return Home to You. I then noticed that more an more people came to plant Your seeds, from which more gigantic Trees of Life sprouted.

Together, we transformed the whole are of dry dead grassland into a lush, green, fertile pasture, dotted with Loving Trees; each a doorway Home.

HS: This dream represents the final acceptance of the truth of Who You Are. It is the end of your lessons here. I will gently raise you up to Me, as you willingly plant what I have given you; allowing it to grow into firm belief and faith. Come under My guidance and allow Me to lead you Home. It is My responsibility and function to do so, and yours is to but accept My help. Defer all things to Me, and all things will lead you down My path.

The following quotations from the Course are from
MANUAL FOR TEACHERS
29. As For the Rest...

"The curriculum is highly individualized, and all aspects are under the Holy Spirit's particular care and guidance. Ask and He will answer. The responsibility is His, and He alone is fit to assume it. To do so is His function. To refer questions to Him is yours." (2:6-10)

"There is another advantage—and a very important one—in referring decisions to the Holy Spirit with increasing frequency." (3:1)

"To follow the Holy Spirit's guidance is to let yourself be absolved of guilt. It is the essence of the Atonement. It is the core of the curriculum. The imagined usurping of functions not your own is the basis of fear. The whole world you see reflects the illusion that you have done so, making fear inevitable. To return the function to the One to Whom it belongs is thus the escape from fear. And it is this that lets the memory of love return to you. Do not, then, think that following the Holy Spirit's guidance is necessary merely because of your own inadequacies. It is the way out of hell for you." (3:1-11)

"To ask the Holy Spirit to decide for you is simply to accept your true inheritance. Does this mean that you cannot say anything without consulting Him? No, indeed! That would hardly be practical, and it is the practical with which this course is most concerned. If you have made it a habit to ask for help when and where you can, you can be confident that wisdom will be given you when you need it. Prepare for this each morning, remember God when you can throughout the day, ask the Holy Spirit's help when it is feasible to do so, and thank Him for His guidance at night. And your confidence will be well founded indeed." (5:4-10)

"Never forget that the Holy Spirit does not depend on your words. He understands the requests of your heart, and answers them. Does this mean that, while attack remains attractive to you, He will respond with evil? Hardly! For God has given Him the power to translate your prayers of the heart into His language. He understands that an attack is a call for help. And He responds with help accordingly." (6:1-7)

"A loving Father does not let his child harm himself, or choose his own destruction. He may ask for injury, but his father will protect him still. And how much more than this does you Father love His son?" (6:9-11)

"Ask all things of His Teacher, and all things are given you. Not in the future but immediately; now. God does not wait, for waiting implies time and He is timeless." (7:6-8)

HS: And it is through acceptance of your role in forgiveness that this world will be transformed at last. The world will be forgiven, and it will come to a peaceful end as it is replaced with your true reality in Heaven.

The following quotations from the Course are from TEXT Chapter 17 — II. The Forgiven World

"The real world is attained simply by the complete forgiveness of the old, the world you see without forgiveness. The great Transformer of perception will undertake with you the careful searching of the mind that made this world, and uncover to you the seeming reasons for your making it. In the light of the real reason that He brings, as you follow Him, He will show you that there is no reason here at all." (5:1-3)

"All this beauty will rise to bless your sight as you look upon the world with forgiving eyes. For forgiveness literally transforms vision, and let's you see the real world reaching quietly and gently across chaos, removing all illusions that had twisted your perception and fixed it on the past. The smallest leaf becomes a thing of wonder, and a blade of grass a sign of God's perfection." (6:1-3)

HS: Let the truth take deep hold within your heart and be healed this holy instant. You need only step back and allow Me to lead you. Follow Me, for I know the Way to your peace.

Chapter 30: Lessons 361-365

Each Of Us Is A Gift To One Another

361. This holy instant would I give to You. Be You in charge. For I would follow You, Certain that Your direction gives me peace.

HS: The holy instant is the moment you surrender all your control, all your judgment, and all your thoughts about the world, to God. Give them all to Him through your small willingness to admit that you have been wrong about everything. Put down your sword. Ask Him to be in charge, for you know not what you do, nor to Whom you do it. Follow Him instead of following your own choices and your own decisions. These are all based upon false presumptions. Only He knows the truth, so gladly put Him in charge. Choose to follow Him, and be certain His direction will give you peace.

362. This holy instant would I give to You. Be You in charge. For I would follow You, Certain that Your direction gives me peace.

HS: Give each instant of your life over to God. Move into a state of "perpetual forgiveness" as you surrender to the truth; you want only what lies beyond perception. Ask that God be in charge of all your thoughts and clear a space for Him, through your humble admission that you do not want what you see, nor do you understand it. Follow only Him, above all else. Be certain that His direction will give you peace.

363. This holy instant would I give to You. Be You in charge. For I would follow You, Certain that Your direction gives me peace.

HS: Choose to give every instant to God, by refusing to accept what your eyes show you. This will transform the world around you into a holy place as you lay a white lily of forgiveness in the place of each form of separation you look upon. Gradually, the soft green pastures and beautiful Tree of Life will begin to grow as you go the way of peace.

364. This holy instant would I give to You.
Be You in charge. For I would follow You,
Certain that Your direction gives me peace.

HS: And so, the beginning and the end now meet, as all lessons come full circle, returning to where we began:

Lesson 1: Nothing I see in this room [on this street, from this window, in this place] means anything.

Nothing you see around you means anything, because it is all an illusion, representing the original thought of separation from God. None of it is real. You cannot assume you know what anything is, because you see it incorrectly. Understand that in seeing just one thing as it truly is, you will have forgiven the world. Forgiving a coffee cup or a pencil may the hardest thing you ever do. All forms of separation have manifested from your original choice to separate from God, and so, by forgiving them, you make another choice. This is the path that leads you Home. Give each holy instant to God, as you choose to follow Him; certain that His direction gives you peace.

365. This holy instant would I give to You.
Be You in charge. For I would follow You,
Certain that Your direction gives me peace.

Words are no longer necessary now, as you move into deepest silence. Be at peace, knowing only this is true; you are God's holy Son and will be forevermore.

And now, with faith and trust, do I ask you to wholly give yourself over to Me.

Amen.

. . .

ME: Amen. Wow. I never realized that the lessons all hooked together like this, coming back full circle to the beginning again.

HS: They are a single cohesive thought system, designed to open your mind, expand your awareness, and awaken you to the truth.

ME: I don't really feel all that different actually.

HS: Don't let that fool you. You *are* different. Nobody who takes the Course remains unchanged, unhealed or feeling unreal. You can never go back to who you were before, and you cannot unlearn what you know now. There is no such thing as "regression" once these lessons have been undertaken, despite how things may appear on the outside or how poorly you felt you went through them. The fact you had the willingness to try, is enough to bring healing to your mind. You don't need to keep doing them over and over again either, attempting to experience some divine revelation. That is not necessary. Once is enough. After that, you may do them again, simply for the pleasure the words and ideas bring you. No formal method need be followed. Apply these lessons to your life as I direct you.

ME: Oh that's a relief. I've heard of people who've done these lessons multiple times, and I wondered how many times it would take me to achieve enlightenment. It seemed like I had a lot of work ahead of me.

HS: No ritual or sacrifice is asked, only a small willingness to accept the truth of Who You Are.

ME: I feel like in order for me to accept the truth of Who I Am, it's going to take a *lot* of willingness. Understanding myself in relationship to All That Is still seems impossible.

HS: It is not impossible. In fact, it is already done. Your journey to Me is the but a remembrance of what and where you have always been.

The following quotation from the Course is from TEXT Chapter 8 — VI. The Treasure of God

"We cannot be separated. Whom God has joined cannot be separated, and God has joined all His Sons with Himself. Can you be separated from your life and your being? The journey to God is merely the reawakening of the knowledge of where you are always, and what you are forever." (9:3-6)

HS: The holy instant will come to you, and everyone; that much I promise. Simply love one another, as I have loved you. Each of your brothers is a divine messenger of Mine that I have specifically sent to you; each is My gift to you. Each of you comes to one another, bearing the message of your holy relationship in Me.

The following quotations from the Course are from TEXT Chapter 20 — V. Heralds of Eternity

"In this world, God's Son comes closest to himself in a holy relationship." (1:1)

"So do the parts of God's Son gradually join in time, and with each joining is the end of time brought nearer. Each miracle of joining is a mighty herald of eternity." (1:5-6)

"Each herald of eternity sings of the end of sin and fear. Each speaks in time of what is far beyond it." (2:1-2)

"Peace to your holy relationship, which has the power to hold the unity of the Son of God together." (2:5)

"It is impossible to overestimate your brother's value." (3:1)

"Judge not what is invisible to you or you will never see it, but wait in patience for its coming." (3:5-6)

"This is no gift your brother's body offers you. The veil that hides the gift hides him as well. He *is* the gift, and yet he knows it not. No more do you." (7:5-8)

ME: Thank You for these words. This whole conversation has been wonderful. I love You so much. Thank you for Your kind patience, gentle wisdom, and Your steady guidance. Thank You for the gifts You send me in everyone I meet or think of.

HS: Now I leave you with this: To love your brethren as I have loved you. Love without condemnation, without judgment. Love without exclusion, without limit, and without fear. Know that My love for each of you is eternal and unchanging. There is nothing you can do to separate from Me, nor depart from My Presence. I am, and will forever be yours, and you are Mine. We are One Love.

ME: I will put forward my best willingness to love and serve just as You ask.

. . .

As a last gift, I was given the following "prayer." It is from me to you dear reader; a declaration of my determination to remember the essence of why we are here, and what it is we are asked to do. Let us awaken to One Love together.

The Forgiveness Prayer

God loves you.
Of this I am absolutely sure.
God loves you
And therefore so must I
Because I am One with Him.
I love you
As deeply and completely as God loves you,
Though I seem to have forgotten it.
I do not yet see Us as One Spirit,
And therefore I do not know I love you
As God loves you.
I can accept this through forgiveness
For now,
Knowing my vision will one day be corrected
As I practice loving you as God Loves you.
I also know
That you must love me in return
Because you are One with Him as well.
You and I,
We go together.
For I cannot go without you
Because you are part of me.
We are One in God's holy Sonship.
To hold these thoughts
Within our minds
Is to know
That we look upon the face of Christ
In everyone we meet or think of.
Let us love one another
As God does.
And all will be healed
within and without.
This is true forgiveness.
Amen

Author Biography

Beth Geer's spiritual background is rich and diverse. She has had a multitude of psychic, paranormal, and deeply profound spiritual experiences throughout her life, beginning around the tender age of 5. She comes from a dedicated Catholic upbringing, but has also practiced tarot reading for over twenty years, is a Reiki Level II practitioner, and performs various psychic and medium functions for friends and family.

Though her religious and spiritual background appears to be contradictory, it is this very contrast that has given her an unusual open-mindedness towards God and life. Her spiritual life has now taken a dramatic turn, because something extraordinary has suddenly begun to unfold. Several years ago, after over a decade of studying *A Course in Miracles*, she began to hear the Voice of the Holy Spirit open up within her, unlocking a powerful message from Him that she is deeply compelled to share with all of us. Beth promises that this message is simple and easy to understand, and that it will change your life forever. Once you hear this message, you won't be able to go back to your old way of being, or look at the world the same again. It is a happy message of love, healing, spiritual transformation, and awakening. Beth doesn't mean to spoil the ending; but everything's going to be okay. Yes, for every last one of us.

Beth lives in a log home on a forty acre hobby farm in rural Minnesota, with her husband Paul, their two children Miranda and Samuel, along with several horses, too many cats, a moderate flock of chickens, one red footed tortoise, some hamsters, and a dog named Freya; who appears to be a loving Rottweiler, but is actually just a very hairy person with four legs. Beth is a pharmacist by day, and in her free time, when not tending to family or animals, she works on extending a message of healing to the world. She currently holds free monthly classes, geared towards hearing your own Inner Voice through deep-guided meditation, based upon the teachings contained in *A Course in Miracles*.